# Covenant By Sacrifice

# Covenant By Sacrifice

## by Ruth Rieder

Covenant By Sacrifice

All artwork drawn by Wade Plemons

*Unless otherwise indicated, all Scripture quotations are taken from the King James Version of the Bible.*

ISBN: 0-9674360-1-X
First printing: July 2001—5,000 copies

**FOR INFORMATION CONTACT:**
**Ruth Rieder**
**P. O. Box 15252**
**Rio Rancho, NM  87174**

Please visit our Web site @ www.positivepowerofholiness.com
On-line ordering and credit charging available for all products at this address

Printed in the United States by:
Morris Publishing
3212 East Highway 30
Kearney, NE  68847
1-800-650-7888

Dedicated to my beloved husband,
Rev. G. Michael Rieder.

Thank you for allowing me to use your extensive study notes on *psuche* and *zoe*. I thank the Lord for putting our lives together. Your ministry in the Word has fed my soul and opened my understanding to the deep things of the Spirit.

You are my "once in a lifetime" love.

# Acknowledgments

**I bow before my Lord, the Master of the universe in humble adoration of Your supreme power and holiness. You are the center and circumference of my life and my desire is to please You above all else! Thank You for the wondrous privilege of being Your child. May I never do anything to defame Your lovely Name or bring shame to the family into which You have adopted me.**

**MY PRECIOUS DAUGHTERS, Angelica and Miriam:** I thank the Lord for bringing you to our house. Thank you for being patient when Mom writes her books. You bring such joy to me. May you always be women of God! I love you!

**DONNA TEN EYCK:** Words cannot express how thankful I am that the Lord brought you into my life as my friend and prayer partner. Thank you for all that you have invested into my life and this book. You are my "one in a million" friend.

**JERRY AND DARIE SCOTT and THE ARMOR BEARERS PRAYER TEAM:** Thank you for the diligent prayer support. What a comfort to know that each of you is holding me up with prayer, for we can do nothing without God. Thank you for involving Him in this ministry on a continual basis!

**WADE PLEMONS:** Your artistic ability is a true gift from God. But more than that, it is coupled with the anointing. Thank you for the awesome artwork. The hand of the Lord truly has drawn through your pencil.

**BETHANY SLEDGE:** What a pleasure it is to work with you. Thank you for bringing this manuscript to completion in preparation for printing. You do such excellent work!

I want to take a moment to express my deep gratefulness for being nurtured and trained by godly parents. Mom and Dad, you taught me by word and example to love the Lord with all my heart, mind, soul, and strength. You have modeled friendship with Jesus.

# Table of Contents

# Foreword

Ruth Rieder has proven her ability to write with her first two books, *Power Before The Throne* and *Reflecting The Glory*. Now her third book, *Covenant By Sacrifice*, has rolled off the printing press and becomes a challenge to every one of us.

As I pondered her writings, I thought of two very thought-provoking statements. One is "The Deceptiveness of the Gradual" and the other is found in Hebrews 2:3, **"How shall we escape, if we neglect so great salvation."** Drifting is an unconscious process; most of the time one drifts toward the precipice before it is realized. Thus a gradual drifting away from the moorings.

In this book, she brings us back far upstream to the beginnings and to the basics of the Pentecostal experience. Many do not realize what is happening and accordingly are not where they one time were.

The disciples would probably have said, **"This**

*is an hard saying; who can hear it? . . . From that time many of his disciples went back, and walked no more with him. Then said Jesus unto the twelve, Will ye also go away?"*

I urge you to read this book prayerfully and let God's love provide the transportation back to the old paths.

— Cleveland M. Becton

# Introduction

During the process of publishing my first book, *Power Before The Throne*, the Lord spoke to me in prayer regarding this book. After receiving the title and the design for the front cover, I was led on a journey of discovery into the life of Abraham. His path parallels our walk with God, for Romans 4:12 speaks of those *"who also walk in the steps of that faith of our father Abraham."* This journey of sacrifice, stimulated by his love for God and faith in God, led Abraham to the ultimate relationship with his Master—*"he was called the Friend of God."*

Let us consider the differences between Lot and Abraham. Lot pitched his tent toward Sodom while Abraham removed his tent and built an altar in Hebron. The well-watered plains looked so inviting, and Lot did indeed prosper, gaining material blessings. Meanwhile, Abraham journeyed the rocky road of covenant sacrifices in his quest for the "true riches." Developing a covenant relationship with God is a process of altar building and sacrifice. Either we progress toward the world as did Lot or we move closer to God through sacrifice, following in the steps of faithful Abraham.

If you observe these two men through natural eyes, Lot's choice will appear much more convenient and conducive to success; still in the end he lost everything. By contrast Abraham prospered in the Spirit as well as the natural. Losing nothing, he saw the promises of God fulfilled.

Becoming the "Friend of God" will exact a high price from anyone who truly desires to attain this place of blessing. Jesus outlined the cost in John 15:14, where He stated, *"Ye are my friends, if ye do whatsoever I command you."* Many have embarked on this pilgrimage only to be deterred and turned back as each sacrifice became more costly. Nevertheless, God is looking for a "Covenant People" who will do whatever it takes to become His friends and ultimately His chosen bride.

In this book we explore the steps of Abraham as he journeyed toward the fulfillment of the promise. Often we wonder at his willingness to offer up Isaac, yet that decision was the result of many other choices made prior to this ultimate time of testing.

Jeremiah 17:10 declares, *"I the LORD search the heart, I try the reins, even to give every man according to his ways, and according to the fruit of his doings."* God explored every crevice of the heart of Abraham to insure the promised blessing could be entrusted into Abraham's keeping. Likewise, He will examine the heart of every saint of God in order to be certain that we are indeed *"called, and chosen, and faithful."*

The questions your heart must answer are: "Which path will I follow? Will I set my sights on the well-watered plains of this carnal world? Am I seeking for fleshly gratification here and now, or will I remove my tent and commence to offer the necessary sacrifices as I journey down the road that points to friendship with God and the fulfillment of covenant promises?" Your choice will determine your destiny.

Walk with me if you will in the steps of faithful Abraham. . . .

# The World of the Wheel

Ur of the Chaldees was situated in the Fertile Crescent along the banks of the mighty Euphrates River. It was part of the most ancient cradle of civilization, located in a great arc of richly irrigated land not far removed from the Persian Gulf. A defensive wall approximately two-and-one-half miles in circumference offered protection to the inhabitants who dwelt within the precincts. Its religious center, dominated by a ziggurat, was situated near the center of the city. The ziggurat towered over the horizon and had an adjoining court, which served as both the marketplace and religious meeting ground. Beyond the temple complex, where the average people lived, the streets of Ur seemed to meander in a rather haphazard fashion.

The housing of the local citizenry varied according to space and wealth considerations; however, archaeologists have found the same "model house" plan repeated over several centuries in ancient Mesopotamia. A typical house in Abraham's day was two stories tall and had from ten to twenty rooms. The front entrance opened into a small lobby. That entryway opened into a courtyard, which was surrounded with rooms that were used as work areas and sleeping quarters for the servants. Sleeping and leisure accommodations for the resident family were located on the second floor.

The houses were built of thick, unbaked mud walls, which provided warmth during the winter and natural insulation against the heat of summer. When the mud bricks were plastered and whitewashed, the walls appeared somewhat similar to the modern stucco houses.

In the days of Abraham, there were reading, writing, and arithmetic much like today. They learned the multiplication and division tables and even worked the square and cube root. Although the inhabitants of Ur were quite sophisticated in many ways, they were also very superstitious and especially religious. The Mesopotamians invented some four thousand deities.

Hundreds of them might be worshiped in any given city, but each city had one chief god.

Nanna (also called Sin), the moon god, was worshiped as chief deity of Ur. A shrine to this god was located at ground level beside the ziggurat. The adjoining court of Nanna was the marketplace and social center of the city, its surrounding walls housing rooms for storage and priestly lodging. The gateway on the south side of the wall surrounding the ziggurat was the king's seat of judgment, where he attended to legal matters. Other buildings provided additional housing, storage, and worship centers.

Abraham's people were expected to worship the deities and were taught that their purpose in life was to serve the gods. A burgeoning priesthood was developed to facilitate their worship and service in the temples. Caring for the gods included feeding them, and the priests presented food to the statues each day, a "great meal" in the morning and a "light meal" in the evening. After placing food on a table in front of the statue, the priest drew a curtain, enabling the god to eat and wash his hands in private.

Each home had a private chapel or a personal shrine dedicated to their patron god. As in the temple, the deity had to be fed, a task usually assigned to a son of the homeowner. Because of their deep-rooted superstitions, the people of Ur buried figurines and statues under the thresholds of their homes in order to ward off evil spirits. They also wore amulets or good luck charms to protect themselves from the fears of the moment.

These people of yore viewed life as an immortal, wheel-like pattern that was predictive of mortal life. Mortality was nothing more than cyclical patterns ending in death, living in a sea of undulating despair with no hope of eternal life. The gods decided their destinies in life. One's fate was written in the stars and could not be changed.

The age-old words of Black Elk embody the mind-set of the culture of these primitive peoples: *"Everything an Indian does is in a circle, and that is because the power of the world always works in circles, and everything tries to be round. In the old days when we were a strong and happy people, all our power came to us from the sacred hoop of the nation. . . . Even the seasons form a great circle in their changing, and always come back again to where they were. The life of a man is a circle from childhood to childhood and so it is in everything where power moves."*

This circular wheel-like pattern was embodied in the worship of the moon. No figure in heaven was more important than the moon, which was born, waxed, waned, and died as we do. Several symbols dominate ancient art and reflect their belief systems. One of those symbols is the spiral, which represented the cyclical nature of reality. It embodied the phases of the moon, the changing of the seasons, the ever turning wheel of birth, childbearing, and death.

The moon cult was centered in Ur. Fertility rites of "sacred couplings" were a staple of their heathen rituals. Nanna-Sin was male, so female priestesses called "Qadishtu" staffed his temple. Visits to these temple prostitutes were necessary in order to ensure fertility. The way to success was founded in fulfilling the duties of one's sacred cult. This provided the only insurance against the ill will of the gods.

The height of celebration in the city of Ur was the New Year festival. Along the meandering streets of Ur, worship of Mesopotamia's multiple gods escalated to a fevered pitch. Worshipers would struggle to catch a glimpse of the religious processions making their way to the temple complex at the center of the city. Sounds of raucous merrymakers filled the air as the circuit of another year was completed and another cycle loomed on the horizon. Grotesque and frenzied fertility rites dominated the night, while the people of Ur sought for hope. Hope that went beyond the pale of the faceless dark and foreboding moon that governed their lives and decided their destinies. There was no joyful expectation, just the ever turning circular course in the world of the wheel. Would life always continue in this revolving pattern of pointless rituals, or would someone find a way of escape from the clutches of hopelessness? Who would shatter the paradigm and change the world of the wheel?

# The Divine Summons

*The God of glory appeared unto our father Abraham, when he was in Mesopotamia, before he dwelt in Charran, and said unto him, Get thee out of thy country, and from thy kindred, and come into the land which I shall shew thee. Then came he out of the land of the Chaldaeans, and dwelt in Charran: and from thence, when his father was dead, he removed him into this land, wherein ye now dwell.*"[1]

As life continued in its usual course within the city of Ur, something was about to happen that would forever change the course of human history. The complete details of the actual event are shrouded from our eyes. All we know is one day in the midst of the old, habitual cycle of life one man received a divine call to begin a journey into the great unknown, a journey of relationship, a journey of sacrifice.

*"By faith Abraham, when he was called to go out into a place which he should after receive for an inheritance, obeyed; and he went out, not knowing whither he went."*[2]  In the midst of an idolatrous society filled with many gods, Abram made a choice to follow a God he knew nothing about.  It was only a voice; nevertheless, the summons was so imperative that Abram obeyed.  The impact of his calling affected his extended family and they decided to make the journey with him.  *"And Terah took Abram his son, and Lot the son Haran his son's son, and Sarai his daughter in law, his son Abram's wife; and they went forth with them from Ur of the Chaldees, to go into the land of Canaan; and they came unto Haran, and dwelt there."*[3]

It is interesting to note that Terah influenced the clan to stop in Haran, where they remained until he died.  Haran was an important caravan city and a more peaceful part of the Mesopotamian world.  Moreover, the principal deity of Haran was Nanna-Sin, the moon god which Terah had worshiped in Ur.  It was a society where he would have felt at home, for beyond Haran lay the vast, unknown territory of Canaan.

In His infinite mercy, God allowed Abram to remain with his father in Haran until he died; then once again the summons came. This time the call was accompanied by an amazing promise. *"Now the LORD had said unto Abram, Get thee out of thy country, and from thy kindred, and from thy father's house, unto a land that I will shew thee: and I will make of thee a great nation, and I will bless thee, and make thy name great; and thou shalt be a blessing: and I will bless them that bless thee, and curse him that curseth thee: and in thee shall all families of the earth be blessed. So Abram departed, as the LORD had spoken unto him; and Lot went with him: and Abram was seventy and five years old when he departed out of Haran. And Abram took Sarai his wife, and Lot his brother's son, and all their substance that they had gathered, and the souls that they had gotten in Haran; and they went forth to go into the land of Canaan; and into the land of Canaan they came."[4]*

Two extended households were on the move again. Looking over their shoulders to the eastern horizon the last thing they saw was the ziggurat of Haran, mankind's bold attempt to reach into the heavens. No matter how unassuming this excursion into the wilderness may have looked to the casual observer, its leader carried with him a promise that someday would result in his ability to truly touch heaven.

"So *'wayyelekh Avram'* (Abram went)–two of the boldest words in all literature. They signal a complete departure from everything that has gone before in the long evolution of culture and sensibility. Out of Summer, civilized repository of the predictable, comes a man who does not know where he is going but goes forth into the unknown wilderness under the prompting of his God. Out of Mesopotamia, home of canny, self-serving merchants who use their gods to ensure prosperity and favor, comes a wealthy caravan with no material goal. Out of ancient humanity, which from the dim beginnings of its consciousness has read its eternal verities in the stars, comes a party traveling by no known compass. Out of the human race which knows in its bones that all its striving must end in death, comes a leader who says he has been given an impossible promise. Out of mortal imagination comes a dream of something new, something better, something yet to happen, something–in the future."[5]

The first step had been taken in a long journey of discovery. One man finally decided to break the cycle and separate himself from the old way of life. Abram answered the divine summons and went out. . . .

# <u>Chapter Two Footnotes</u>:

1. Acts 7:2-4

2. Hebrews 11:8

3. Genesis 11:31

4. Genesis 12:1-5

5. *The Gifts of the Jews*, Thomas Cahill (Nan A. Talese / Anchor Books, a division of Random House, Inc., New York) page 63.

# The Sacrifice of Separation

*H*<small>earken</small> *to me, ye that follow after righteousness, ye that seek the L<small>ORD</small>: look unto the rock whence ye are hewn, and to the hole of the pit whence ye are digged. Look unto Abraham your father, and unto Sarah that bare you: for I called him alone, and blessed him, and increased him."*[1]

The biblical narrative of Abram becomes much more powerful and poignant when examined against the historical backdrop of the civilization in which he lived. Many times we shy away from examining the heathen society that dominated the ancient world and bequeath sainthood on him prematurely. Abram was very much a heathen worshiper before God called him out of Ur of the Chaldees. This truth is borne out in Joshua 24:2, *"And Joshua said unto all the people, Thus saith the L<small>ORD</small> God of Israel, Your fathers dwelt*

*on the other side of the flood in old time, even Terah,*
*the father of Abraham, and the father of Nachor: and*
<u>*they served other gods.*</u> *"*

When Abram left Ur and Haran, he took more
than just his family and belongings. He also took the
mind-set of his culture on this pilgrimage into un-
charted territory. Each sacrifice God asked of Abraham was designed to sever his connection with the old
way of idolatrous living and create a new thought
pattern.

In like manner, when we are called upon to separate from our old way of life and follow God, we bring
with us the vanity of our worldly minds. That is why
the apostle Paul commanded us, *"Be not conformed to*
*this world: but be ye transformed by the renewing of*
*your mind, that ye may prove what is that good, and*
*acceptable, and perfect, will of God."*[2] Our minds
must also be transformed as we journey toward friendship with God. The sacrifices God requires of us are
intended to separate us from the influences and asso-
ciations of this present evil world.

Amazingly, the society of ancient Mesopotamia
was not too far removed from the mind-set of the hedo-
nistic world in which we find ourselves. Our society
is reverting to the ways of the ancient pagan cultures.

Although there are many modern conveniences and high-tech toys, heathenish spirits are on the rampage. We have simply become "high-tech" heathens.

Just walk through a large shopping mall. See the bizarre clothing and strange haircuts. This is nothing new. It is amazing that many of the same hairstyles worn by the young people of this generation are found in ancient pagan cultures such as the Canaanites.

Continue your trek through the mall. Stores that appeal to children are filled with weird creatures and demonic looking toys. A monitor displays the latest Hollywood blockbuster while posters filled with hideous apparitions greet your eyes. People avidly purchase the latest Hollywood has to offer.

Athletic stores are filled with sports star memorabilia. You can pay homage to your favorite sports heroes by purchasing their jerseys and hats. Neckties and Christmas ornaments imprinted with their logos are also available. Surrounded by merchandise you can cluster around the television to watch the game and cheer on your sports idols.

Finally there is the New Age store offering "good luck" charms and the latest crystals catering to the superstitions of the masses. An in-house tarot card reader is available to tell your fortune or sell you the latest horoscope predictions.

This is similar to the practice of the heathen who worshiped multiple gods in many grotesque shapes and sizes. The likenesses of their gods were worn around their necks and on their bodies as they worshiped in the coliseums and temples. Dark superstitions governed their lives, causing them to wear amulets and bury idols under the thresholds of their homes.

A walk through the mall is like walking through a pagan marketplace. It is no different than the heathen temple complexes of long ago where worship and commerce joined hand in hand. Many voices and choices bombard us on every side. The cacophony of cadences continually confronts us. We must exercise caution so as not to become desensitized to the danger of consorting with the spirits of the age.

Let us draw another interesting parallel between Abram's society and ours. Every Mesopotamian home contained a family shrine, which housed their idols. Worship revolved around these shrines and in this way idolatrous religion thrived at the grass roots level. A portion of each day was dedicated to the ritual of feeding the household gods.

Likewise the homes of this modern era have set up shrines to the gods of Hollywood, fashion, sports, and every perverted lifestyle imaginable. This enables these idolatrous practices to survive and maintain their influence over society. Even those with limited means refuse to do without their entertainment center. Much time is set aside daily to feed their gods.

It has been interesting to observe the grip that television has in the lives of many people as it controls their daily routines. The flickering images of the entertainment world parade through their lives from the beginning of their days until the lights go out at night. Day in and day out this shrine enslaves them. What kind of church would we be if we were as addicted to our one true God as they are to their god?

While I visited a Swedish furniture store, the salesman relayed an interesting bit of information. He said, "In Sweden the home revolves around the kitchen. But in America, the home revolves around the entertainment center." How true that is. In fact, if you do not have a television set, people are astonished.

One day a cable man came to our door asking us to subscribe to his television cable product. My husband informed him that we do not have a TV. Gaping with a befuddled stare, the salesman questioned him as to this strange phenomenon. Shaking his head in disbelief, he walked away in total shock, wondering that anyone would choose not to have that idolatrous shrine in his home.

Deuteronomy 7:25-26 declares: ***"The graven images of their gods shall ye burn with fire: thou shalt not desire the silver or gold that is on them, nor take it unto thee, lest thou be snared therein: for it is an abomination to the LORD thy God. Neither shalt thou bring an abomination into thine house, lest thou be a cursed thing like it: but thou shalt utterly detest it, and thou shalt utterly abhor it; for it is a cursed thing."***

God commands His people to destroy the gods of the heathen that would become a snare to enslave and eventually destroy us. The Word of God enjoins us to refrain from setting up abominations in our houses. There is no room in the temple of God for two altars.[3] His Word declares, ***"Thou shalt have no other gods before me."***[4] We cannot compromise in this decree from the throne of God.

Every abomination to God can be seen not only on television but also on the Internet. Such things as human sacrifice (abortion), homosexuality, idolatry, witchcraft, dishonesty, pride, pornography, murder of innocent lives, wicked imaginations, discord, vengeance, adultery, fornication, and cursing are displayed, and people's feet are running swiftly to partake in this mischief and debauchery. The voices of perversion and sin pervade the media, seeking to influence the choices of our society.

We are familiar with the old argument, "But there are so many good educational programs on television." In Genesis 2:9 and 17, the forbidden tree is called "the tree of the knowledge of **GOOD AND EVIL**"! It is fascinating to observe how many of man's innovations created for good somehow become polluted with evil.

Here are just a few examples:

➤ **telephone:** from the convenience of communication **to** 900-numbers and obscene phone calls

➤ **camera:** from family portraits **to** pornography

➤ **radio:** from family entertainment **to** risqué news bulletins and indecorous programs

➤ **VCR:** from home videos **to** X-rated productions

➤ **books:** from education **to** smut romances

➢ **medicine:** from healing **to** euthanasia and abortion

➢ **Internet:** from the information superhighway **to** propagating every vile perversion known to mankind

Tracing the trail back to the tree in the garden, we find the cause of corruption. Since the day man ate of the tree, his good has become corrupted by evil.

Immoral times demand that holiness transcend the legislative mode of the past. Depravity is escalating daily and confronting the church on every side, making it impossible to compile a comprehensive list encompassing every pitfall. In order to survive in the midst of this crooked and perverse generation, we must obey Paul's injunction in Ephesians 5:15 to walk circumspectly, which means to be careful to consider all the circumstances and the subsequent consequences.

Entering into a relationship of commitment with God is imperative. This enables us to discern between good and evil. Progressing beyond being governed by a list of "dos and don'ts" to a love relationship with the Lord empowers us to withstand in this evil day. We must willingly separate ourselves from anything that would defile our relationship with God.

The doctrine of separation is the oldest doctrine in the Bible. It was instituted back in the Garden of Eden when God instructed Adam and Eve not to partake of the tree of knowledge of good and evil. God asked Abram to separate himself from his country, his kindred, and his father's house. Moses and the Israelites had to be willing to forsake Egypt. Peter left his fishing nets to become a fisher of men. Matthew quickly abandoned the Roman tax collector's booth to follow the call of Jesus. Moreover, the divine summons still echoes the same message even throughout this modern era in which we live. *"Wherefore come out from among them, and be ye separate, saith the Lord, and touch not the unclean thing; and I will receive you, and will be a Father unto you, and ye shall be my sons and daughters, saith the Lord Almighty."*[5]

The covenant of separation is still the initial sacrifice each of us must be willing to make. When a person walks into the church of the living God, the first thing he usually notices is God's separated people. When confronted with a decision, the foremost question everyone must ask himself or herself is, "Am I willing to forsake all to be His disciple?" That is always the inaugural step in a journey of relationship with God.

It is like the woman who goes shopping for a new dress in an exclusive boutique. Finding one that looks pleasing, she runs her hand down the sleeve, looking for the price tag. The price usually determines the purchase. If we are not willing to pay the price of separation from the world, then we will never be set free from the hopeless cycle of eternal damnation.

The covenant relationship was contingent upon Abram's obedience and the acceptance of separation. One of the key words in Abram's life is separation. He was from first to last a separated man. Separated from Ur and Haran, separated from Lot, separated from the customs of the old life, separated from the people around him. Likewise the call has gone forth in each of our lives bidding us to come out and be separate, touching not the unclean thing.

As long as a bird remains in the nest it will never know the luxury of flight. If a surfer remains on the shoreline fearfully flirting with the tide, he will never know the challenge of catching an ocean wave or the ecstasy of riding it to shore. As long as we cling to the material world, we cannot appropriate the promises of God. Abram could have never become Abraham, the father of the faithful, if he had remained in Ur or Haran. He had to be willing to pay the price of separation and venture forth into the unknown regions of God's call.

God's plan for Abram necessitated total separation from his former lifestyle and the influences that had governed his choices. Setting his sights on that city whose builder and maker is God, Abram stepped out in faith. If we desire to be His disciples, our lives must exhibit the same willingness. Separation from the old life is the first of many sacrifices along the pathway which will lead to friendship with God.

## Chapter Three Footnotes:

1. Isaiah 51:1-2

2. Romans 12:2

3. II Kings 21:4-7; II Chronicles 33:4-7

4. Exodus 20:3

5. II Corinthians 6:17-18

# Guarding the Evening Sacrifice

*A*nd Abram journeyed, going on still toward
the south.*"[1]* One by one the years slipped by, and
God's call to leave Haran seemed long ago. After a
time of sojourning in the land of Egypt, Abram and Lot
decided to go their separate ways. Lot journeyed east
and Abram settled in the plain of Mamre. Life had
been good to Abram and Sarai but there was still no
sign of the promised seed.

Abram had just returned from a victorious raid
on King Chedorlaomer and his league of kings. Succeeding in freeing Lot and his family from bondage,
Abram restored the rest of the captives and their pos-
sessions to the king of Sodom. While sitting inside his
tent he pondered the future. As Abram sat deep in
thought, the Word of the Lord came to him in a vision.

The familiar voice of God assured him saying,

*"Fear not, Abram: I am thy shield, and thy exceeding great reward."*[2] Ever the self-confident, calculating desert chieftain, Abram did not hesitate to voice the question that had been uppermost in his thoughts. He asked the Lord, *"What wilt thou give me, seeing I go childless, and the steward of my house is this Eliezer of Damascus? And Abram said, Behold, to me thou hast given no seed: and, lo, one born in my house is mine heir."*[3]

Immediately the Lord responded, *"This shall not be thine heir; but he that shall come forth out of thine own bowels shall be thine heir."*[4] Leading Abram outside, the Lord told him to look into the heavens and see if he could count the stars. Gazing at the starlit sky, Abram began trying to count the stars. He started at one corner of the sky and commenced counting; then losing track, he started over again.

When Abram gave up in futility, the Lord told him, *"So shall thy seed be. And he <u>believed</u> in the LORD; and he counted it to him for righteousness."*[5]

Seeking further proof of the promised inheritance, Abram asked the Lord for a sign. Once again Abram was summoned to the place of sacrifice. The Lord instructed him to take a heifer, a she goat, and a ram, each being three years old. In addition to the large animals, he was also to take a turtledove and a young pigeon. It was a costly commitment, for when animals mature to the age of three years, they are ready to breed. Only then do they become productive, giving a return on the investment. Willing to consecrate his substance to the Lord, Abram searched through his flocks till he found the very best.

Abram divided the large animals in the middle and laid each piece one against the other, but the birds were left whole. Exhausted and bloody, Abram settled down to await a response from the Lord. According to a primitive practice, the two parties involved in the covenant were to pass through the midst of the slain animals, indicating that if either of them broke the covenant it would fare with him as with the slain and divided beasts.[6]

The day wore on, and as the shadows lengthened into the late afternoon, the smell of blood began to attract the attention of the birds of prey. Circling overhead, the carrion birds sought for an opportunity to dive and consume Abram's sacrifice. When the birds began swooping in to devour the sacrifice, Abram went into action. Driving them back with his staff and waving his mantle, he frightened them away. He could not relax. When he did, the vultures became emboldened to descend upon the slain animals. Drenched in sweat from the exertion of his vigil, his arms ached from weariness.

The ravenous fowls began moving toward the slain birds, seeking a smaller target upon which to prey. These smaller sacrifices were more easily captured; with just one taste, nothing would stop the bloodthirsty fowls from consuming everything in sight. Determining that nothing would defile his sacrifice, knowing his future and the fulfillment of the promise depended upon his pledge, Abram moved quickly to protect the turtledove and pigeon.

Finally, as the sun set, the carrion birds departed, seeking an easier quarry. Abram had won. Exhausted from the struggle, Abram fell into a deep sleep. As he slept, the Lord spoke to him concerning the future of his progeny. At long last, Abram's faithfulness was rewarded. The Lord promised him a long and peaceful life.

Awakening, Abram beheld a most wondrous sight. The Lord passed through the midst of the sacrifice in the form of a smoking furnace and a flaming torch. The fire of God consumed the sacrifice. God took the oath upon Himself; He alone could fulfill the covenant of promise. Abram had successfully guarded the evening sacrifice.  Now he must continue in his faithfulness to God while maintaining the covenant of consecration.

## <u>Chapter Four Footnotes</u>:

1. Genesis 12:9

2. Genesis 15:1

3. Genesis 15:2-3

4. Genesis 15:4

5. Genesis 15:5-6

6. Jeremiah 34:18-20

# Little Foxes

In the saga of Abram's life, Genesis 15:6 introduces a brand-new word. For the first time in Holy Writ, the word *believed* appears. *"And he **believed** in the LORD; and he counted it to him for righteousness."* In the previous verses Abram poured out his soul to God concerning the depths of his heart's desire for a child. Tenderly, the Lord affirmed the promise to Abram's troubled spirit. At that moment he progressed into a place of believing God. Once he believed, his faith demanded action; consequently, the costly evening sacrifice resulted as evidence of his confidence in God. This foreshadowed the blood sacrifices of the Old Testament law, which ultimately pointed the way to the perfect sacrifice.

Believing God is the next step in our covenant relationship with the Lord. *"But without faith it is impossible to please him: **for he that cometh to God must believe** that he is, and that he is a rewarder of* *them that diligently seek him.*"[1]   After separating ourselves from the world, repentance for our sins will result as we put to death the old man.  Traversing the road of redemption, our belief in God will produce a sacrifice in our lives.  Faith always demands action. *"Even so faith, if it hath not works, is dead, being alone."*[2]  It is a costly and bloody experience to put to death the things we once held dear.  Nevertheless, in the wake of our first love, nothing is too good and no price too great!

Yet it is important to remember that making the initial sacrifice is not enough.  We can learn a valuable lesson upon examining the actions of Abram.  Once his sacrifice was made, it had to be diligently guarded.  As the night shadows gathered around Abram, the birds of prey sought to steal his offering to God.

Correspondingly, the day is wearing on and the foul spirits of this age have begun swooping around our sacrifices, seeking to dive in and devour them. They would love to consume those things we have consecrated to the Lord, thereby preventing the covenant from being fulfilled. Thus the battle ensues as the night approaches.  It is time to get out our staff, the Word of God, and the mantle of anointing.  We must drive back the spirits of darkness circling overhead.

Relaxing our vigilance for one moment will give them the opportunity to dive in for the kill.

The first sacrifices targeted by the enemy are the little ones. If satan can devour these, he will be emboldened to assault the larger consecrations in our lives. The enemy understands we cannot be influenced to go out tomorrow and commit gross sin. However, he can lead us into it gradually through a process of desensitization. It could happen quite subtly, should we grow weary in the battle. The following account illustrates this point so poignantly.

In 1936 Margaret Mitchell published a book called *Gone With the Wind*. She was paid $50,000, which at that time was the largest sum ever paid to anyone for a first-time novel. Set against the historical backdrop of the Civil War, it became an award winning best-seller. Shortly after the book's first publication, Selznick International Pictures decided to make the story into a movie. Casting for the screenplay began in July of 1936. Vivian Leigh starred as Scarlett O'Hara while Clark Gable played the part of Rhett Butler. The motion picture was completed on December 9, 1939, and released to the public in January 1940. It went on to win ten Academy Awards.

One small curse word spoken at the end of the

final scene set *Gone With the Wind* apart from any other film ever released. America was scandalized; this type of language had never been used in the national media. However, it was not long before things calmed. After all, it was just one tiny four-letter word, and it seemed to make such an appropriate ending to the story. There was no reason to get overly concerned about one little dirty word. Or was there?

Where did that single, minuscule expletive take us? That seemingly insignificant indiscretion breached the foundation of America's morality. Just over a half century later, the floodgates of filth have been unleashed into our society through the film industry–pornography, sex, violence, filthy language, violent video and virtual reality games. Crime is rising. Criminals are on the rampage. Our young people are driven to rape, kill, and commit suicide. The streets of our cities and the halls of our schools have become unsafe. And to think that it started so insignificantly.

What happened to the great city of Ephesus? Often mentioned in the New Testament, it was one of the cultural and commercial centers of its day. Located at the mouth of the Cayster River, Ephesus was noted for bustling harbors, broad avenues, gymnasiums, baths, a huge amphitheater, and especially the magnificent Temple of Diana. What happened to bring about its gradual decline until the harbor was no longer crowded with ships and the city was no longer a flourishing metropolis?

Was it smitten by plagues, destroyed by enemies, or demolished by earthquakes? No, silt was the reason for its downfall–silent and nonviolent silt. Over the years, fine sedimentary particles slowly filled the harbor, distancing the city from the economic life of the sea traders.

Evil practices and little acts of disobedience may seem harmless; however, let the silt of sin gradually accumulate and we will find ourselves far from God. The writer of Hebrews admonished us, ***"Wherefore seeing we also are compassed about with so great a cloud of witnesses, <u>let us lay aside every weight, and the sin which doth so easily beset us</u>, and let us run with patience the race that is set before us, looking unto Jesus the author and finisher of our faith; who for the joy that was set before him endured the cross, despising the shame, and is set down at the right hand of the throne of God."***[3]

Remember the words of the wise man, Solomon, as he instructed us in the Song of Solomon 2:15, ***"Take us the foxes, the little foxes, that spoil the vines: for*** *our vines have tender grapes.* " Foxes were not overly dangerous, just destructive. They were cunning hunters, eating small animals and birds and having a fondness for certain fruit.[4]

The obvious sins will not cause us to stumble; we are constantly on guard against them. It is the little sins and weights that entrap us, enticing us down the path of compromise. After all, they are just "little foxes." There is no reason to be so concerned over the little indiscretions in our lifestyles. They are just little things and everyone else is doing it. Does it matter? Why must we be so strict and old-fashioned? Are sacrifices we made in the beginning still necessary? Can't we ease up a bit in this new millennium?

*"For our vines have tender grapes."* This is the reason we must protect our vineyards and our covenant sacrifices in these last days. The decisions we make will not only affect us but also have a far-reaching impact upon generations to come. Our children are watching us, and what we allow in moderation, the next generation will do in excess![5] Abram's actions not only impacted him but determined the future of his descendants as well.

It is a frightening thing to see little foxes slinking into the church, becoming accepted, and in some cases even protected. As the old saying goes, "Vice is a monster of such frightful mien, that to be hated needs but to be seen; but seen too oft, familiar with its face, we first endure, then pity, then embrace!" (Pope)

I'm reminded of the story of two fishermen on the reservoir. Caught up in the excitement of the trip, they neglected to put down an anchor upon reaching their desired fishing spot. Oblivious to the subtle undercurrent of the water, they began trolling for fish. As the hours passed, suddenly one of the fishermen looked up. To his startled horror, their boat had drifted dangerously close to destruction. Shouting a warning to his partner, they began rowing with all their might, seeking to escape the deadly rapids that lay just ahead. After an exhaustive and furious effort, they made it safely to shore. The fishermen wondered how they could have drifted so far. It happened imperceptibly. The danger was not detected until it was almost too late.

How easy it is to get caught up in the excitement of the moment–the latest conference, the next church service, the newest hit song, just the routine of serving God. There are things creeping in that we know in our heart of hearts are dangerous. But they seem like such little encumbrances–oh, it is just a little immodesty, a little makeup, a little hair dye, a little fingernail polish, a little jewelry, a little hatred, a little gossip, and the list goes on. Why, it is nothing to worry about. A little bit of the world won't hurt. Or so our human reasoning seems to say as we drift ever so slightly toward shipwreck.

A ship once wrecked on the Irish coast. The captain was a careful one. Nor had the weather been of so severe a kind to explain the wide distance the ship had swerved from her course. The ship went down, but so much interest was attached to the disaster that a diver was sent to investigate.

Among other portions of the vessel that were examined was the compass. When the compass box was swung on deck and opened, a piece of metal was detected. It was very tiny, just a bit of steel which seemed to be the small point of a pocketknife blade. It appeared that the day before the wreck a sailor had been sent to clean the compass, had used his pocket-knife in the process, and unconsciously broke off the point, which was left remaining in the box.

The bit of knife exerted its influence on the compass, to a degree that deflected the needle from its correct bent and spoiled it as an index of the ship's direction. That piece of penknife wrecked the vessel. Thus one trifling sin, one small weight as small as a broken knife point can mess up our sense of direction and send us down the path of destruction.[6]

Not long ago a stranger met an overland traveler, who had walked on foot from the Golden Gate Bridge to New York. He was interested to know what was the greatest difficulty the traveler had encountered in his long journey. He suggested that perhaps the mountains on the trail had been the greatest barrier, but the traveler assured his questioner it was not that. Then he suggested that perhaps the swollen streams, which cut across his road, presented the greatest hazard, but it was not that. After a little he said, "What almost defeated me in my journey across the continent was the sand in my shoes." Life is forever tripping over trivial things.[7]

No, it is not the big diversion that will send us down the path of compromise. It is usually just the subtle curve in the road. More than likely the giant assaults of the enemy will not destroy our consecrations. It will probably be nothing more than . . . little foxes.

# <u>Chapter Five Footnotes</u>:

1. Hebrews 11:6

2. James 2:17

3. Hebrews 12:1-2

4. *Illustrated Manners and Customs of the Bible*, J. I. Packer, M. C. Tenney (Thomas Nelson Publishers, Nashville) page 229.

5. Judges 2:19

6. *Knight's Master Book of New Illustrations*, Walter B. Knight (Wm. B. Eerdmans Publishing Company) page 623.

7. Ibid., page 637.

# Egypt's Son

*Now Sarai Abram's wife bare him no children: and she had an handmaid, an Egyptian, whose name was Hagar.*"[1]

Have you ever stopped to ponder the question of how Hagar came to be a part of Abram's household? To find the answer we must retrace our steps in the Scripture to Genesis 12:10-20.

*"And there was a famine in the land: and <u>Abram went down into Egypt to sojourn there; for the</u> famine was grievous in the land."* When God wrote His Word, He did not disguise the character flaws found within the people through whom He chose to work. This particular portion of Scripture reveals the depth of Abram's self-seeking nature. Severe famine plagued the land; consequently, Abram decided to go down into Egypt to find sustenance.

As their caravan prepared to enter Egypt, Abram asked Sarai to do a very peculiar thing. He knew that the Egyptians liked beautiful women, and even at sixty-five-plus years, Sarai was still a very comely woman. Abram feared the Egyptians would kill him and abduct his wife. In a moment of self-preservation, forgetting the awesome promises of God, he entreated his wife to lie on his behalf. ***"Say, I pray thee, thou art my sister: that it may be well with me for thy sake; and my soul shall live because of thee."***

Ever the obedient wife, Sarai acted according to her husband's request. Sure enough, the princes of Egypt were taken with her beauty and rushed to tell Pharaoh about the latest lovely lady who had traversed their borders. Determined to satisfy his sensual appetite, Pharaoh quickly brought Sarai into his house.

Can you imagine the utter terror she must have felt when she was wrenched from her husband's arms and forced into a heathen harem? Tormenting thoughts must have plagued Abram as he imagined his beloved wife being ravished by another man. Of course, Pharaoh paid him well for the new addition to his royal residence.

***"And he entreated Abram well for her sake: and he had sheep, and oxen, and he asses, and menservants, and <u>maidservants</u>, and she asses, and camels."*** Among the many riches Abram received for this fiasco was a young maidservant that in the years to come would wreak havoc in his home. Pharaoh took Sarai and gave Hagar in return.

Notwithstanding, God was in complete control of Sarai's destiny. She was part of His purpose, and her pining away in the Pharaoh's palace was not part of the eternal plan. *"And the LORD plagued Pharaoh and his house with great plagues because of Sarai Abram's wife."* Pharaoh summoned Abram and rebuked him for his dishonesty. Sarai was restored and they departed from Egypt.

Unfortunately, as a result of Abram's desire to protect himself, the seed for adversity had been planted in his home. It was cleverly concealed, just waiting for the proper time to spring forth and bear bitter fruit. Thus entered Hagar into the household of promise.

*"Now Sarai Abram's wife bare him no children: and she had an handmaid, an Egyptian, whose name was Hagar."* It had been ten years since God's initial promise to make of Abram a great nation. Year after year Sarai had remained barren. In the ancient culture of the Middle East, barrenness was a terrible reproach. If a couple was childless, the woman was always blamed. People of the town would ridicule an infertile woman. Even those who loved her treated her

as an object of pity and placed her in the same category as a widow.

But barrenness was more than a physical or social problem. Deep religious meanings were attached to the problem as well, and barrenness was thought to be a result of disobeying God. It is hard to imagine how devastating this kind of stigma would be for a childless wife in those days. She was psychologically depressed, socially disgraced, and spiritually ruined. A barren couple would spend a good deal of time examining their past failures to see if there was any sin in their lives that had brought about their infertility. When sin was ruled out as a cause of the problem, the wife was free to inquire about different kinds of remedies. She would eat certain foods, such as mandrakes, apples, or fish, that were believed to aid a woman in conception.

Some other common practices included wearing amulets or offering cakes, drink offerings, and burning incense to the queen of heaven (Ashtoreth) who was the Canaanite fertility goddess. If all these remedies were unsuccessful, drastic measures could be taken. A husband could take another wife or the barren wife could use a slave to bear children on her behalf.[2] That is how Sarai came to offer Hagar to her husband. To the western mind, Sarai's actions seem inconceivable; however, surrogate motherhood was a very common practice during patriarchal times.

*"And Sarai said unto Abram, Behold now, the LORD hath restrained me from bearing: I pray thee, go in unto my maid; it may be that I may obtain children by her. And Abram hearkened to the voice of Sarai. And Sarai Abram's wife took Hagar her maid the Egyptian, after Abram had dwelt ten years in the land of Canaan, and gave her to her husband Abram to be his wife. And he went in unto Hagar, and she conceived: and when she saw that she had conceived, her mistress was despised in her eyes."[3]*

It did not take long for trouble to start brewing within the once peaceful home. As soon as Hagar conceived, she began to despise her mistress. Anger flared within Sarai and she immediately blamed Abram for the outcome of her actions. *"And Sarai said unto Abram, My wrong be upon thee: I have given my maid into thy bosom; and when she saw that she had conceived, I was despised in her eyes: the LORD judge between me and thee."[4]*

Now Abram is caught in the middle of two brawling women. Seeking to pacify his distraught wife, he gave her permission to deal with Hagar as she saw fit. *"But Abram said unto Sarai, Behold, thy maid is in thy hand; do to her as it pleaseth thee. And when Sarai dealt hardly with her, she fled from her face."*[5]

Sarai unleashed her pent-up rage on Hagar, causing the servant girl to run away. Finding Hagar by a fountain of water in the wilderness, the angel of the Lord told her to return to Sarai and submit herself. Then the angel foretold the destiny of her child.

*"And the angel of the LORD said unto her, Behold, thou art with child, and shalt bear a son, and shalt call his name Ishmael; because the LORD hath heard thy affliction. And he will be a wild man; his hand will be against every man, and every man's hand against him; and he shall dwell in the presence of all his brethren."*[6]

To this day our world suffers from the ill-fated decision of Sarai to take matters into her own hands. Growing tired of tarrying, she sought to fulfill the miraculous promise through human reasoning and ability. But the arm of flesh cannot procure God's promises. Whenever we seek to do things our way, turmoil will arise, bringing sorrow to succeeding generations.

The Lord gave Abram a barren wife on purpose in order to fulfill His plan in His own time and in His own way. In fact, every one of the patriarchs had a barren wife–Abram and Sarai, Isaac and Rebekah, Jacob and Rachel. While God was promising to multiply their seed and make them into great nations, He gave them unfruitful wives, thereby establishing an eternal principle by which He always works. ***"He maketh the barren woman to keep house, and to be a joyful mother of children. Praise ye the LORD."***[7]

The psalmist declared, ***"Except the LORD build the house, they labour in vain that build it: except the LORD keep the city, the watchman waketh but in vain. It is vain for you to rise up early, to sit up late, to eat the bread of sorrows: for so he giveth his beloved sleep. Lo, children are an heritage of the LORD: and the fruit of the womb is his reward."***[8] There is no reason for us to get up early and sit up late worrying about how God is going to do a mighty work in this end time. If He does not build His church, we are all in trouble. We cannot save anyone or fill one single person with the Holy Ghost. Only the Creator can birth eternal life.

We can learn a lesson from the choices that Abram and Sarai made in this lamentable narrative. When hard times come, as most assuredly they will, we must not go down to Egypt to find food. Throughout the Bible Egypt typifies the world and its fleshly lusts. Egypt always promotes self-preservation. When self is allowed to dictate our decisions, avenues of conception will be introduced into our lives that are at odds with the pure plan of God.

Bringing the fleshpots of Egypt into the church of the living God will never result in the miraculous promise of end-time revival. He does not need Egypt's help to fulfill His eternal purpose. The covenant child will not be born from an illicit union of righteousness and unrighteousness. That is an unequal yoke, and the apostle declared, *"Be ye not unequally yoked together with unbelievers: for what fellowship hath righteousness with unrighteousness? and what communion hath light with darkness? And what concord hath Christ with Belial? or what part hath he that believeth with an infidel? And what agreement hath the temple of God with idols?"[9]*

Please do not grow impatient as you wait on the Lord. *"Be not deceived; God is not mocked: for whatsoever a man soweth, that shall he also reap. For he that soweth to his flesh shall of the flesh reap corruption; but he that soweth to the Spirit shall of the Spirit reap life everlasting. And let us not be weary in well doing: for in due season we shall reap, if we faint not.*"[10]  Growing tired of waiting for the Lord to bring to pass the promised miracle, many have begun to sow to the flesh.  They have gone down to Egypt in search of provision and have come back with an Egyptian bondwoman.  Notwithstanding, what has begun in the Spirit will never be completed in the flesh.  The promised seed will never come by way of Egypt's son!

## Chapter Six Footnotes:

1. Genesis 16:1

2. *Illustrated Manners and Customs of the Bible*, J. I. Packer, M. C. Tenney (Thomas Nelson Publishers, Nashville) pages 441-442.

3. Genesis 16:2-4

4. Genesis 16:5

5. Genesis 16:6

6. Genesis 16:11-12

7. Psalm 113:9

8. Psalm 127:1-3

9. II Corinthians 6:14-16a

10. Galatians 6:7-9

# Covenant by Circumcision

*A*nd when Abram was ninety years old and
*nine, the LORD appeared to Abram."*[1]

Approximately fifteen years had passed since
Abram's last encounter with the Lord in Genesis 15.
It had been a time of waiting and wondering when the
promise would be fulfilled, a period of sovereign silence that continued to perfect the faith of the patriarch. At last, *"when Abram was ninety years old and
nine,"* the Lord appeared to him, bringing a new covenant and greater revelation of Himself. *"I am the Almighty God; walk before me, and be thou perfect.
And I will make my covenant between me and thee,
and will multiply thee exceedingly."*[2]

Seeing the splendor of God and receiving an
invitation to greater intimacy with the Almighty caused
Abram to fall on his face. Reverently he listened as

God continued speaking of the impending promises. Reaffirming the covenant between them, the Lord said, ***"As for me, behold, my covenant is with thee, and thou shalt be a father of many nations. <u>Neither shall thy name any more be called Abram, but thy name shall be Abraham; for a father of many nations have I made thee</u>. And I will make thee exceeding fruitful, and I will make nations of thee, and kings shall come out of thee."***[3]

Each heavenly visitation brought God's plan into clearer focus. In Haran, the promise was ***"I will make of thee a great nation."***[4] Bethel brought the assurance that God would ***"make thy seed as the dust of the earth."***[5] During the vision in Mamre the Lord declared, ***"Look now toward heaven, and tell the stars, if thou be able to number them . . . So shall thy seed be."***[6] Now the patriarch is told that he will be ***"a father of many nations."***[7]

Names were of extreme importance in those days, and Terah had given his eldest son a name to live up to–Abram or *Exalted Father*. This name embodied Terah's dream for his son, a name designed to motivate him to become a leader. Even without children Abram could fulfill his father's aspiration for his son to become an exalted leader among men. However, God's plan would far surpass his father's desires. No longer would this chosen man be called Abram but Abraham, meaning *Father of a multitude.*

By custom, the receipt of a new name in the eastern world symbolized new life. Signifying a new or amplified purpose, it was the highest honor bestowed upon a man. After many years of emptiness, Abraham was given a new beginning. Only God had the power to create and fulfill every design determined for Abraham's life.

The Lord continued talking to Abraham and he listened with wonder as God promised the land of Canaan unto him and his seed for an everlasting possession. *"And I will establish my covenant between me and thee and thy seed after thee in their generations for an everlasting covenant, to be a God unto thee, and to thy seed after thee. And I will give unto thee, and to thy seed after thee, the land wherein thou art a stranger, all the land of Canaan, for an everlasting possession; and I will be their God."*[8]

At this juncture in the Scripture, God revealed the token of obedience necessary to insure the fulfillment of the covenant promises. *"This is my covenant, which ye shall keep, between me and you and thy seed after thee; Every man child among you shall be circumcised. And ye shall circumcise the flesh of your foreskin; and it shall be a token of the covenant betwixt me and you. And he that is eight days old shall be circumcised among you, every man child in your generations, he that is born in the house, or bought with money of any stranger, which is not of thy seed. He that is born in thy house, and he that is bought with thy money, must needs be circumcised: and my covenant shall be in your flesh for an everlasting covenant. And the uncircumcised man child whose flesh of his foreskin is not circumcised, that soul shall be cut off from his people; he hath broken my covenant."*[9]

Abraham and his God were to establish an unbreakable bond, which in this period were always contracted in blood, usually the blood of animal sacrifices. But God took the covenant to a new level of sacrifice. The blood of this bond was to be Abraham's own and that of *"every man child among you."* From this day forward in every generation the token of circumcision would be the sign of the covenant. In this manner, the children of Abraham would be virtually unable to forget the God who never forgets them. Disobedience to God's command carried a heavy penalty of punishment involving separation from God and His people. The promises were contingent on Abraham's submission to the requirements of God.

Then the Lord addressed Sarai and her role in the covenant fulfillment. No longer called Sarai or *Princess*, her name was changed to Sarah, meaning *A mother of nations*. This pronouncement of blessing upon his wife brought overwhelming disbelief, causing Abraham to fall on his face and laugh as he said in his heart, *"Shall a child be born unto him that is an hundred years old? and shall Sarah, that is ninety years old, bear?"*[10]

Seeking an easier way for God to fulfill His promises, Abraham offered the solution of his Egyptian son, Ishmael. *"And Abraham said unto God, O that Ishmael might live before thee!"*[11] Emphatically God responded, *"Sarah thy wife shall bear thee a son indeed; and thou shalt call his name Isaac: and I will establish my covenant with him for an everlasting covenant, and with his seed after him."*[12] God would never need a human solution to fulfill His divine plan, for He *"calleth those things which be not as though they were."*[13]

Graciously the Lord pronounced a blessing upon Ishmael. Nevertheless the covenant would be established with Isaac, the son whom Sarah would bear unto

Abraham at the foreordained time in the next year. With those words, the Lord finished talking with Abraham and departed from him.

Before the sun went down, Abraham carried out God's commandment in its entirety. *"And Abraham took Ishmael his son, and all that were born in his house, and all that were bought with his money, every male among the men of Abraham's house; and circumcised the flesh of their foreskin* <u>*in the selfsame day*</u>*, as God had said unto him."*[14]

*"And Abraham was ninety years old and nine, when he was circumcised in the flesh of his foreskin. And Ishmael his son was thirteen years old, when he was circumcised in the flesh of his foreskin. In the selfsame day was Abraham circumcised, and Ishmael his son. And all the men of his house, born in the house, and bought with money of the stranger, were circumcised with him."*[15] Fulfilling the covenant of circumcision, the process of transformation was continuing to unfold in the heart and life of Abraham, the "father of the faithful."

# <u>Chapter Seven Footnotes</u>:

1. Genesis 17:1

2. Genesis 17:1-2

3. Genesis 17:4-6

4. Genesis 12:2

5. Genesis 13:3, 16

6. Genesis 15:5

7. Genesis 17:5

8. Genesis 17:7-8

9. Genesis 17:10-14

10. Genesis 17:17

11. Genesis 17:18

12. Genesis 17:19

13. Romans 4:17

14. Genesis 17:23

15. Genesis 17:24-27

# Obedience = Love
# Love = Obedience

The writings of Paul clearly communicate Old Testament circumcision represents the rite of baptism and putting away the sins of the flesh. *"In whom also ye are circumcised with the circumcision made without hands, in putting off the body of the sins of the flesh by the circumcision of Christ: buried with him in baptism, wherein also ye are risen with him through the faith of the operation of God, who hath raised him from the dead. And you, being dead in your sins and the uncircumcision of your flesh, hath he quickened together with him, having forgiven you all trespasses."*[1]

The covenant process through which God led the patriarch foreshadows the New Testament plan of salvation. First he believed and made the required animal sacrifice in Genesis 15, which represents repentance.

Next he is circumcised in Genesis 17, a typology of baptism. This mirrors the command of Jesus found in Mark 16:16, *"He that believeth and is baptized shall be saved; but he that believeth not shall be damned."*

The token of circumcision became the dividing line in Abraham's life and in the lives of his descendants. Throughout the ages this sign would set them apart from the heathen world Abraham had left behind. God carved in His people an unmistakable reminder of the holy relationship into which they had entered. Correspondingly, baptism in Jesus' name identifies and separates us from this present evil world when the sins of the flesh are put off. Baptism in Jesus' name for the remission of sins is essential to insure salvation even as circumcision was fundamental to the Abrahamic covenant. The seriousness of God's commandment behooves us to be diligent and instill this wondrous truth in our children from generation to generation.

Embodied in the act of circumcision were separation, purity, and obedience. Likewise, baptism separates the believer from past sins which are remitted and washed away by the blood of Jesus in the watery grave. Peter identified the reason we submit and obey the command to be baptized, *"The like figure whereunto even baptism doth also now save us (not the putting* away of the filth of the flesh, <u>but the answer of a good</u> <u>conscience toward God,</u>) by the resurrection of Jesus Christ. *"*[2] The confidence of a clear conscience is the end result of our obedience.

The impact of Abraham's unwavering and swift obedience to God's command can be seen throughout the entire Hebrew race. To this day the ritual of circumcision lives on in his descendants. In the New Testament church this word actually became synonymous with the Jews who were identified as "the Circumcision." Through baptism Gentile believers become the "spiritual Circumcision," *"For we are the circumcision, which worship God in the spirit, and rejoice in Christ Jesus, and have no confidence in the flesh."*[3]

The rite of circumcision became a source of utmost pride among the Jewish nation. Sadly the ritual was passed on, but the humility and obedience of Abraham was not exhibited among his progeny. They came to love the ritual while forgetting its purpose and the God who instituted it. To the same extent baptism in Jesus' name can become a point of pride if we go through the ritual of spiritual circumcision while forgetting the underlying purpose is to manifest our obedience and love for God.

To correct this problem yet another spiritual

operation must take place within the heart of every believer. *"And <u>the LORD thy God will circumcise thine heart, and the heart of thy seed</u>, to love the LORD thy God with all thine heart, and with all thy soul, that thou mayest live."[4]* Love is the missing ingredient. When love is absent, formal rituals will ensue, strangling joyous obedience. Heart circumcision will produce all-consuming love, thereby bringing eternal life, and love is much more uncompromising than law.

Abraham's love and obedience caused the Lord to make an amazing statement concerning him in Genesis 18:17-19: *"And the LORD said, Shall I hide from Abraham that thing which I do; seeing that Abraham shall surely become a great and mighty nation, and all the nations of the earth shall be blessed in him? <u>FOR I KNOW HIM</u>, that he will command his children and his household after him, and they shall keep the way of the LORD, to do justice and judgment; that the LORD may bring upon Abraham that which he hath spoken of him."*

Abraham's willingness to obey everything the Lord asked of him resulted in divine confidence. No hint of hesitation or unwillingness was ever displayed in Abraham's action. As Abraham trod the path of covenant relationship with the almighty God, no sacrifice was too costly or painful. Thus God was enabled to fulfill His ultimate plan and purpose within this man of faith.

Today talk is cheap! People repeatedly profess their love for God. But when the cost of obedience looms before them, they form a god in their own image. A dishonest heart will produce an idol fashioned after your own lusts that does not require a costly sacrifice. Isaiah said it like this, ***"Wherefore the Lord said, Forasmuch as this people draw near me with their mouth, and with their lips do honour me, but have removed their heart far from me, and their fear toward me is taught by the precept of men."***[5]

The precepts of men produce nothing more than lip service as the propaganda of "easy believism" is embraced and perpetuated. This diabolical doctrine falsely labels obedience to God's precepts as legalism. People who live a holy, separated life or "walk the talk" are derisively called "LEGALIST, LEGALIST." However, here is food for thought. Webster's definition of legalism is *"Strict adherence to law."* Hmm, maybe being a "legalist" is not such a bad thing after all.

Such a hostile reaction is usually the result of a

convicted conscience. The standard line of defense is that an obedient person is lacking in the love of God. Far too many people confuse being loving with remaining silent about sin. In many religious circles the definition of love is "I'm okay and you're okay." "If you love me, do not confront my sin." That is a distorted definition of love. If I truly love you, I will tell you the truth because I Corinthians 13:6 declares charity *"rejoiceth not in iniquity, but rejoiceth in the truth."* By the same token the wise man, Solomon, instructed us, *"Faithful are the wounds of a friend; but the kisses of an enemy are deceitful."*[6] A person who refuses to tell you the truth does not really love you no matter what flowery fleshly platitudes he spouts in an attempt to seduce your soul.

At a certain meeting after a powerful revelatory message was preached on holiness, another speaker got up and said, "I'm for holiness and all that stuff, but what we really need is love." The enemy continually uses this ploy to intimidate the church, trying to shut our mouths.

Is it possible to have one without the other? According to the Word of God, what is the true definition of love? Is it this sweet, syrupy version that is being trumpeted on every side? What does it really mean to love the Lord our God with all our heart, mind, soul, and strength and our neighbor as ourselves?

Here is God's definition of love:

➤ *"If ye love me, keep my commandments"* (John 14:15).

➤ *"He that hath my commandments, and keepeth them, he it is that loveth me: and he that loveth me shall be loved of my Father, and I will love him, and will manifest myself to him"* (John 14:21).

➤ *"Jesus answered and said unto him, If a man love me, he will keep my words: and my Father will love him, and we will come unto him, and make our abode with him. <u>He that loveth me not keepeth not my sayings</u>: and the word which ye hear is not mine, but the Father's which sent me"* (John 14:23-24).

➤ *"If ye keep my commandments, ye shall abide in my love; even as I have kept my Father's commandments, and abide in his love"* (John 15:10).

➢ *"But whoso keepeth his word, in him verily is the love of God perfected: hereby know we that we are in him"* (I John 2:5).

➢ *"For this is the love of God, that we keep his commandments: and his commandments are not grievous"* (I John 5:3).

➢ *"And this is love, that we walk after his commandments. This is the commandment, That, as ye have heard from the beginning, ye should walk in it"* (II John 6).

In light of these Scriptures, we can safely conclude that love is equivalent to obedience. Obedience is how we manifest our love for God and to God. Do we not exhibit our love for our spouses through our actions? Should it be any different with God? Assurance of salvation is found in loving God and remaining obedient as we walk after His commandments. If we do not love God, we will find a way to justify our disobedience. ***"He that loveth me not keepeth not my sayings."***[7]

Now the question becomes, "How do I manifest love to the family of God?" Once again the answer is found in God's Word. *"By this we know that we love the children of God, when we love God, and keep his commandments."*[8] Our love and obedience to God reveals our love for one another. If I am walking in disobedience I do not love you. It does not matter what kind of verbiage I express with my lips. It is much easier to say the right thing than to do the right thing.

Paul admonished in Galatians 5:13-14, *"For, brethren, ye have been called unto liberty; only use not liberty for an occasion to the flesh, but by love serve one another. For all the law is fulfilled in one word, even in this; Thou shalt love thy neighbour as thyself."* Love for my fellow saint will govern the choices that I make. Serving one another in love will keep us from doing anything that would give an occasion to stumble.

In an era of "political correctness" the church is confronted with the pitfall of "religious correctness." The only way to be "religiously correct" is to align our lives and message with the Word of God. Jesus stated in Matthew 5:20, *"For I say unto you, That except your righteousness shall exceed the righteousness of the scribes and Pharisees, ye shall in no case enter into the kingdom of heaven."*

According to this Scripture, entrance to the kingdom is found in exceeding the meticulous righteousness of the scribes and Pharisees. Unfortunately, the Pharisees were caught up in making sure every detail of the outward man was correct while neglecting the inner man. Pride governed their actions instead of love for God.

Seeking to escape Phariseeism, many religious people today have gone to the other extreme, professing what is on the outside does not matter–it is the inside that counts. Both of these philosophies are erroneous. Jesus gave the correct balance in Matthew 23:26, *"cleanse first that which is within the cup and platter, that the outside of them may be clean also."* A clean heart will manifest itself in the outer man.

I Samuel 16:7 is often taken out of context and interpreted incorrectly by many false teachers. *"But the LORD said unto Samuel, Look not on his countenance, or on the height of his stature; because I have refused him: for the LORD seeth not as man seeth; for man looketh on the outward appearance, but the LORD looketh on the heart."* Excusing their own lack of obedience, those who shun outward holiness and decry its necessity flippantly quote this verse.

Consider with me the consequences of God's

looking on the heart of an individual. The story of Ananias and Sapphira in Acts 5 is a classic example of God looking beyond the outward appearance to the heart of the matter. To the eyes of man, it appeared as if this couple was doing a noble thing. Yet God read their hearts and discerned their dishonest motives. When God examined their hearts it resulted in death. Truly God sees not as man sees. He knows why we are disobedient and discerns the hidden motivation behind all we do or do not do.

God does indeed care about the outer man as well as the inner man. Paul exhorted in Romans 12:1-2, *"I beseech you therefore, brethren, by the mercies of God, that ye present your bodies a living sacrifice, holy, acceptable unto God, which is your reasonable service. And be not conformed to this world: but be ye transformed by the renewing of your mind, that ye may prove what is that good, and acceptable, and perfect, will of God."* This Scripture portrays both components necessary for true holiness–holy bodies and transformed minds.

Holiness is not a club in the hand of the church used to beat God's bride into submission. Holiness is not negative–holiness is positive! When we become holy, we become like God. Apostle Peter said it like this, *"But as he which hath called you is holy, so be ye holy in all manner of conversation; because it is written, Be ye holy; for I am holy."*[9]

Let us consider the next verse: *"And if ye call on the Father, <u>who without respect of persons</u> judgeth according to every man's work, pass the time of your sojourning here in fear."*[10] Peter first made this statement concerning "respect of persons" in Acts 10:34, *"Then Peter opened his mouth, and said, Of a truth I perceive that God is no respecter of persons: but in every nation he that feareth him, and worketh righteousness, is accepted with him."* The door of salvation has been thrown wide open that whosoever will may come and drink of the water of life freely.

God is no respecter of persons when it comes to redemption. Neither is He a respecter of persons when it comes to holiness. God expects all of His children to be obedient to His Word regardless of their culture, color, or race. When we come into His kingdom, racial barriers are totally torn down. *"For he is our peace, who hath made both one, and hath broken down the middle wall of partition between us."*[11]

Paul wrote in Galatians 3:27-28, *"For as many of you as have been baptized into Christ have put on Christ. <u>There is neither Jew nor Greek</u>, there is* *neither bond nor free, there is neither male nor female: for ye are all one in Christ Jesus.*" Again he declared in Colossians 3:10-11, *"And have put on the new man, which is renewed in knowledge after the image of him that created him: where <u>there is neither Greek nor Jew, circumcision nor uncircumcision, Barbarian, Scythian,</u> bond nor free: but Christ is all, and in all.*" Ethnicity is eradicated in the body of Christ.

As the words of a favorite children's song express, "Red and yellow, black and white, they are precious in His sight." God is not prejudiced in any way and so requires **all** His children to obey His Word. Ethnic heritage and culture will never justify disobedience in anyone's life. Each of us will be judged without "respect of persons" because we are now part of His holy nation. Citizenship in this kingdom transcends all other cultures. In light of this Peter enjoined us to *"pass the time of your sojourning here in fear."*

Galatians 5:6 sums up this chapter so beautifully, *"For in Jesus Christ neither circumcision availeth any thing, nor uncircumcision; but faith which worketh by love."*

The effectiveness of your faith is dependent on the depth of your love for the Master. Love is the

overflowing source of joyful obedience.
Obedience + Love = Faith!

## Chapter Eight Footnotes:

1. Colossians 2:11-13

2. I Peter 3:21

3. Philippians 3:3

4. Deuteronomy 30:6

5. Isaiah 29:13

6. Proverbs 27:6

7. John 14:24

8. I John 5:2

9. I Peter 1:15-16

10. I Peter 1:17

11. Ephesians 2:14

# Child of Promise

*And the LORD visited Sarah as he had said, and the LORD did unto Sarah as he had spoken. For Sarah conceived, and bare Abraham a son in his old age, at the set time of which God had spoken to him. And Abraham called the name of his son that was born unto him, whom Sarah bare to him, Isaac.*[1]

Disbelieving laughter resounded from the lips of Abraham when God told him of the impending birth. In response God chose the name for the miracle child– Isaac, meaning *laughter*. Sarah also laughed incredulously within herself upon learning of the promised son. Abraham laughed, Sarah laughed, but now God had the last laugh as the elderly couple held the tangible evidence of God's laughter in their arms–Isaac, child of promise. *"And Sarah said, God hath made me to laugh, so that all that hear will laugh with me."*[2]

*"And Abraham circumcised his son Isaac*

*being eight days old, as God had commanded him. And Abraham was an hundred years old, when his son Isaac was born unto him. . . . And the child grew, and was weaned: and Abraham made a great feast the same day that Isaac was weaned.*"[3]   Joyous celebration reverberated through the household of Abraham and Sarah.   However, an undercurrent of trouble was brewing in the midst of the gaiety.  Before the day ended, Abraham would be called on to make yet another sacrifice.

*"And Sarah saw the son of Hagar the Egyptian, which she had born unto Abraham, mocking."*[4] Hostility welled up in Ishmael's heart because of the intrusion of this "new" son.  Bursting forth in mocking contempt, he began making fun of Isaac.  As he did, the wrath of Sarah was kindled and she entreated Abraham to send away the bondwoman and her son.  Years of contention finally demanded a response.

*"Wherefore she said unto Abraham, Cast out this bondwoman and her son: for the son of this bondwoman shall not be heir with my son, even with Isaac."*[5]

A sudden pall descended over the feast as Abraham's heart grieved over Sarah's request. *"And the thing was very grievous in Abraham's sight because of his son.*"⁶ The merriment of the moment began to diminish as one by one the guests departed, leaving Abraham with a momentous decision to make. What should he do? He loved Isaac with a depth of love he had never before realized or thought possible. Yet on the other hand, he dearly cherished his firstborn son, Ishmael. His heart felt as if it was being torn into a million pieces. Why must life be so complicated?

As Abraham's mind whirled in circles, he heard the familiar voice of the Almighty. *"And God said unto Abraham, Let it not be grievous in thy sight because of the lad, and because of thy bondwoman; in all that Sarah hath said unto thee, hearken unto her voice; for in Isaac shall thy seed be called."*⁷

Once more the broken man of God traversed the difficult road of consecration. *"And Abraham rose up early in the morning, and took bread, and a bottle of water, and give it unto Hagar, putting it on her shoulder, and the child, and sent her away: and she departed, and wandered in the wilderness of Beersheba."*⁸ Giving bread and water to Hagar, the old patriarch drew Ishmael to him one last time as their tears of suffering mingled together. Then somehow Hagar found the courage to begin the trek away from the only home Ishmael had ever known.

Watching Ishmael walk away, Abraham felt as if his heart would break. As he gazed into the distance, Ishmael and Hagar grew smaller and smaller until finally they were lost from view. Even though the pain of Ishmael's absence continued to haunt Abraham, he obeyed the voice of God.

*"For it is written, that Abraham had two sons, the one by a bondmaid, the other by a freewoman. But he who was of the bondwoman was born after the flesh; but he of the freewoman was by promise. Which things are an allegory."*[9] The sons of Abraham represent two religious groups—one born of the flesh, the other born of the Spirit.

Born of a bondwoman after the flesh, Ishmael could boast nothing miraculous of his birth. It was the result of human impatience and resourcefulness. When God chose not to operate according to man's time clock, they tried to help Him by producing their own solution.

Egypt's son was a half-breed—right father, wrong mother. It mattered who his mother was because his mother would choose his wife. *"And his mother took him a wife out of the land of Egypt."*[10] Hagar chose a woman just like herself for her son—she chose another Egyptian.

There is a religious group born after the flesh with nothing miraculous in their spiritual birth. Eagerly "accepting Christ as personal savior," their "salvation plan" is a product of human ingenuity. Why should they wait for the *"promise of the Father"* when a humanistic solution can be manufactured? That outdated promise is no longer in operation today, or so they say. The mother of this half-breed church is an Egyptian bondmaid. Using the Word of God and professing to know Him, they continue living like Egypt and partake of its merchandise. While promising liberty, they are entangled with the beggarly elements of the world, *"which gendereth to bondage, which is Agar."*[11]

*"But Jerusalem which is above is free, which is the mother of us all. For it is written, Rejoice, thou barren that bearest not; break forth and cry, thou that travailest not: for the desolate hath many more children than she which hath an husband. NOW WE, BRETHREN, AS ISAAC WAS, ARE THE CHILDREN OF PROMISE"!*[12]

Born of a miraculous birth, Isaac was God's will in human form, an ever present reminder of the intangible presence of the Creator. No greater manifestation of the reality of God could have been asked for. This child embodied the earnest of the inheritance that was to come–seed like the sands of the seashore and stars in the sky.

What a beautiful picture of redemption's plan is portrayed in this supernatural birth. We were dead in trespasses and sins, *"having no hope, and without God in this world."*[13] But in His due time resurrection power flowed through us and brought forth the miracle of the new birth. We have received the precious promise of the Father, *"which is Christ in you, the hope of glory."*[14]

Our mother is Jerusalem, the true church. Born of the Spirit, the offspring of liberty, we have been set free from the bondage of Egypt. *"Wherefore thou art no more a servant, but a son; and if a son, then an heir of God through Christ."*[15]

By miraculous means we became children of promise when *"God . . . sent forth the Spirit of his Son into your hearts, crying, Abba, Father."*[16] The Holy Ghost is a continual reminder of the invisible God. It is the earnest of our inheritance–eternal life.

➤ *"Now he which stablisheth us with you in Christ, and hath anointed us, is God; who hath also sealed us, and <u>given the earnest of the</u>*

*Spirit in our hearts"* (II Corinthians 1:21-22).

➤ *"Now he that hath wrought us for the selfsame thing is God, who also hath <u>given unto us the earnest of the Spirit</u>"* (II Corinthians 5:5).

➤ *"In whom ye also trusted, after that ye heard the word of truth, the gospel of your salvation: in whom also after that ye believed, <u>ye were sealed with that holy Spirit of promise, which is the earnest of our inheritance until the redemption of the purchased possession, unto the praise of his glory</u>"* (Ephesians 1:13:14).

*"But as then he that was born after the flesh persecuted <u>him that was born after the Spirit</u>, even so it is now."*[17]   Just as Ishmael persecuted Isaac, the world church persecutes the true church. Labeling us a cult or people in bondage, they actually proclaim a false message and are held captive by their own fleshly lusts.

Let us never become intimidated or compromise our One God, apostolic message. *"We, brethren, as Isaac was, are the children of promise."*[18] The inheritance belongs to us! Why are we going to Ishmael, the world church, seeking ways to claim our inheritance? Crowding their facilities full of people seeking an easy path, they are nothing more than a product of human ingenuity. The Lord does not desire a worldly crowd but a sanctified church. They cannot teach us how to build churches! Only God can build His church! *"Upon this rock I will build my church; and the gates of hell shall not prevail against it."*[19]

*"Nevertheless what saith the scripture? Cast out the bondwoman and her son: for the son of the bondwoman shall not be heir with the son of the freewoman."*[20] It is time to cast Egypt out of our midst. We do not need Egypt's ways or methods! The early church turned the world upside down through prayer, fasting, miracles, signs, wonders, and preaching the Word. They did not need slick packaging and marketing techniques. Herein lies the secret to their success: *"And they went forth, and preached every where, the Lord working with them, and confirming the word with signs following. Amen."*[21] If it worked back then, it will still work today because Jesus Christ is *"the same yesterday, and to day, and for ever."*[22]

Compromising our message of holiness and flooding our churches with worldliness will never enable us to claim our inheritance! It will cause us to lose our birthright. As the children of Israel prepared to pass through the waters of the Red Sea, Moses made a profound statement of faith. *"And Moses said unto the people, Fear ye not, stand still, and see the salvation of the LORD, which he will shew to you to day: <u>for the Egyptians whom ye have seen to day, ye shall see them again no more for ever.</u>"*[23] When we pass through the waters of baptism, the Egyptians that held us captives are drowned in the sea of forgetfulness. The world and all its lusts are left behind. We must never invite Egypt back into our lives!

There is no place for Egypt in God's kingdom. Egypt's son shall never be heir with the child of promise. *"So then, brethren, we are not children of the bondwoman, but of the free."*[24] Don't ever get a case of mistaken identity and forget who we are:

***<u>NOW WE, BRETHREN, AS ISAAC WAS, ARE THE CHILDREN OF PROMISE!</u>***

## Chapter Nine Footnotes:

1. Genesis 21:1-3

### *Covenant By Sacrifice*

2. Genesis 21:6

3. Genesis 21:4-5, 8

4. Genesis 21:9

5. Genesis 21:10

6. Genesis 21:11

7. Genesis 21:12

8. Genesis 21:14

9. Galatians 4:22-24

10. Genesis 21:21

11. Galatians 4:24

12. Galatians 4:26-28

13. Ephesians 2:12

14. Colossians 1:27

15. Galatians 4:7

16. Galatians 4:6

17. Galatians 4:29

18. Galatians 4:28

19. Matthew 16:18

20. Galatians 4:30

21. Mark 16:20

22. Hebrews 13:8

23. Exodus 14:13

24. Galatians 4:31

# The Ultimate Sacrifice

*A nd Abraham planted a grove in Beersheba, and called there on the name of the LORD, the everlasting God. And Abraham sojourned in the Philistines' land many days."*[1] Following the departure of Hagar and Ishmael, life began settling into a peaceful pattern. Abraham planted a grove of trees and tarried in Beersheba many days. The years passed and the anguish of Ishmael's departure became less acute. As Abraham poured himself into the rearing of Isaac, the bonds of love grew stronger between the father and his remaining son.

As Isaac matured into manhood, Abraham realized anew the many sacrifices God required of him had been well worth it. Secure in the fulfillment of the promise of Isaac, no doubt remained in Abraham's mind. Everything else God had promised would surely come to pass. Life was good as the elderly patriarch sat by the well within the shady grove and listened to the infectious laughter of the promised child. Surely the testing had come to an end with the climax of Ishmael's departure.

One by one the Almighty had removed every idol from Abraham's heart; however, one idol yet remained. God had to know one more thing about the man of faith. *"And it came to pass after these things, that God did tempt Abraham, and said unto him, Abraham: and he said, Behold, here I am."*[2] Eagerly Abraham waited to hear what God would say, but His next words almost turned Abraham to stone. *"And he said, Take now thy son, thine only son Isaac, whom thou lovest, and get thee into the land of Moriah; and offer him there for a burnt offering upon one of the mountains which I will tell thee of."*[3]

With stark simplicity the story of Abraham's final testing unfolds in the Word of God. The Author permits the reader to mentally fill in the blanks of emotional upheaval that surely must have assaulted the devoted father. For the first time in Scripture, God uses the word *lovest*. This word poignantly illustrates the depth of Abraham's devotion for his only son. Did he initially feel outrage, fright, rebellion, or hatred toward the Lord? We will never fully know the extent of Abraham's emotions until each of us is summoned to this place of ultimate sacrifice.

Heaven held its breath as the aged patriarch reasoned within himself. Reaching the place of surrender, Abraham began preparing for the journey. He could not forget God's unwavering faithfulness to him and once again he answered the summons to the place of sacrifice. *"And Abraham rose up early in the morning, and saddled his ass, and took two of his young men with him, and Isaac his son, and clave the wood for the burnt offering, and rose up, and went unto the place of which God had told him."*[4]

After three days they entered the foothills of the land of Moriah. Abraham saw the dreaded hill in the distance. When they arrived at the base of the mountain, Abraham briefly instructed the young servants to wait with the donkey. *"And Abraham said unto his young men, Abide ye here with the ass; and I and the lad will go yonder and <u>worship,</u> and come again to you."*[5] What a wondrous expression is the word *worship*. Even in the midst of the testing, God deserved adoration and worship. It reflects the mood of the patriarch's mind. He was absorbed with the One who had sent him forth on this sorrowful errand.

With utmost confidence, Abraham told the young men he **and the lad** would <u>return</u>. *"And Abraham took the wood of the burnt offering, and laid it upon Isaac his son; and he took the fire in his hand, and a knife; and they went both of them together."*[6] Lifting the bundle of wood and laying it on Isaac's back, he took the firepot and knife. Together they began the climb to the top of Mount Moriah.

As they climbed, Isaac questioned his father about the apparent absence of a sacrifice. Abraham simply answered, *"My son, God will provide himself a lamb for a burnt offering: so they went both of them together."*[7] Still closer they came to the dreaded summit.

*"And they came to the place which God had told him of; and Abraham built an altar there, and laid the wood in order, and bound Isaac his son, and laid him on the altar upon the wood."*[8] Upon reaching the mountain peak, Abraham set about building an altar. Isaac looked on as he arranged the wood. Unable to put off the dreaded moment any longer, Abraham told his son what God required of him. Willingly Isaac allowed his father to bind him and lay him on the altar. Resolutely Abraham picked up the knife as he prepared to offer his greatest treasure. He must never forget

Isaac did not really belong to him. He was God's gift to Abraham, a promise entrusted into human keeping.

All the other sacrifices had prepared Abraham for this moment–the supreme test of his faith. Years of molding, shaping, and designing led the patriarch to this ultimate sacrifice. This time God could not help him; it was Abraham's test, his moment of victory or defeat. Before him was the door upon which human history would swing. This moment of moral choice would inscribe the pages of the future. At this juncture, a man would decide the course of human events, for the Lord had entrusted the power to him.

In absolute surrender to the will of the Almighty, Abraham lifted his arm; the hand that held the dagger prepared for its powerful descent. Isaac tensed and closed his eyes as he waited for the force of the descending knife. On the foreboding crest of Moriah, two dismal, pathetic figures stood under the watchful eye of their God. An unearthly silence enveloped the scene as time stood still.

At that moment a voice thundered from heaven. *"ABRAHAM, ABRAHAM."* With his glinting dagger poised in midair, Abraham hoarsely answered, *"Here am I."*[9] Then came the most wondrous words the aged patriarch had ever heard: *"Lay not thine hand upon* the lad, neither do thou any thing unto him: <u>**FOR NOW I KNOW**</u> **that thou fearest God, seeing thou hast not withheld thy son, thine only son from me.**"[10]

Trembling, the old arm fell lifeless to the father's side, the knife slipping unnoticed to the ground. A dead man dropped that deathly blade. Someone died there on Mount Moriah, but it was not Isaac. Abraham, the proud father, ambitious for and possessive of his beloved son and heir to all his personal desires, chose instead to become alive to the will of God. **Every vestige of idolatry was completely cleansed from his heart.**

*"And Abraham lifted up his eyes, and looked, and behold behind him a ram caught in a thicket by his horns: and Abraham went and took the ram, and offered him up for a burnt offering in the stead of his son."*[11] Quickly Abraham removed the bonds from Isaac and together they offered up the ram in sacrifice to God. From the lofty heights of Moriah, Abraham looked across the vale of the centuries and saw the day of Jesus Christ, the perfect sacrifice that was to come. *"Your father Abraham rejoiced to see my day: and he saw it, and was glad."*[12]

*"And Abraham called the name of that place* <u>*Jehovah-jireh*</u>*: as it is said to this day, In the mount*

*of the LORD it shall be seen.* "[13] This is a true saying. The provision of the provider will not be obtained until we approach the place of sacrifice. God does not bring deliverance until we reach the point of our greatest need. When our Isaac is on the altar and the knife is about to descend, God's angel will intervene.

God had often promised, but for the first time He swore by an oath by Himself, the highest authority in the universe. *"And the angel of the LORD called unto Abraham out of heaven the second time, and said, By myself have I sworn, saith the LORD, for because thou hast done this thing, and hast not withheld thy son, thine only son: that in blessing I will bless thee, and in multiplying I will multiply thy seed as the stars of the heaven, and as the sand which is upon the sea shore; and thy seed shall possess the gate of his enemies; and in thy seed shall all the nations of the earth be blessed; <u>because thou hast obeyed my voice.</u>* "[14]

As Abraham and Isaac wended their way down the mountain, the patriarch's face reflected the inner tranquility of one who had sacrificed all unto the faithful God only to find himself richer, having lost nothing. The father of the faithful had passed the test, and the covenant promises could be totally entrusted into his keeping. *"And the scripture was fulfilled which* saith, **Abraham believed God, and it was imputed unto him for righteousness:** <u>*AND HE WAS CALLED THE FRIEND OF GOD.*</u> "[15]

## <u>Chapter Ten Footnotes:</u>

1. Genesis 21:33-34

2. Genesis 22:1

3. Genesis 22:2

4. Genesis 22:3

5. Genesis 22:5

6. Genesis 22:6

7. Genesis 22:8

8. Genesis 22:9

9. Genesis 22:11

10. Genesis 22:12

11. Genesis 22:13

12. John 8:56

13. Genesis 22:14

14. Genesis 22:15-18

15. James 2:23

# The Kingdom of Self

The key to understanding the majestic story of Abraham's lofty mountaintop trial does not lie in his relationship with Isaac but in his relationship to God. At the offset Abraham was a man of Mesopotamia, a polytheist who believed in many gods and goddesses. For this man of heathen origins, the gods were nothing more than statues sitting in a family shrine. Charms and amulets worn for good luck were part of his idolatrous worship. God called Abraham out of this life of idolatry and in the process had to change his concept of the Creator.

From voice, to vision, to divine manifestation, Abraham's comprehension of the omnipotent One came into clearer focus. With each covenant sacrifice He came to the realization that the almighty God was not like the statues he had previously worshiped who were replete with human attributes. After all the years of tutelage and mind transformation, the mountaintop experience was the climatic revelation of the supreme Potentate. At this point God became the ultimate Ruler of Abraham's heart. This God was worthy of his complete devotion and no sacrifice was too great, not even his beloved son. Abraham finally understood that God was in total control of his destiny. His task was simply to say, "Here I am!" as he completely surrendered his heart and soul to the Master.

The epic of Abraham is simply an example and pattern of God's dealings in each of our lives. We too have been called *"out of darkness into his marvellous light"*[1] and our entire thought process must be transformed. Each part of our spiritual metamorphosis is essential to our newfound relationship with the Lord: separation, repentance, baptism in Jesus' name, the infilling of the Holy Ghost, and living a consecrated life. Progressing along the same pathway of promise enables us to *"grow in grace, and in the knowledge of our Lord and Saviour Jesus Christ."*[2]

You have probably been enjoying the journey and the road has not been too difficult. Nevertheless, if your true desire is to reach the place where God becomes the ultimate Lord of your life, you must be willing to traverse Moriah's forbidding slopes. Only in the lonely mountaintop experience can total surrender be found. Ultimate obedience is rooted in the relinquishment of your most precious treasure–yourself. This is the ultimate sacrifice, the death of that old, selfish soul life you cling to so ferociously.

Are you willing to obey Him at any cost? Then listen for the Master's call. If you can pass this test and offer up the kingdom of self, covenant blessings await!

Where did the sovereignty of self originate? It started way back in the Garden of Eden. *"And the LORD God formed man of the dust of the ground, and breathed into his nostrils the breath of life; and man became a living soul."*[3] Life was idyllic in this place of perfection. It was an earthly paradise. One commandment was given to mankind: *"And the LORD God commanded the man, saying, Of every tree of the garden thou mayest freely eat: but of the tree of the knowledge of good and evil, thou shalt not eat of it: for in the day that thou eatest thereof thou shalt surely die."*[4]

At first glance this precept may seem rather simple to obey. Lamentably, obedience does not come easily to the natural man. Everything was fine until the serpent reared its ugly head. *"Now the serpent was more subtil than any beast of the field which the* LORD *God had made. And he said unto the woman, Yea, hath God said, Ye shall not eat of every tree of the garden?"*[5]

Immediately satan attacked the weakest area, their self-seeking nature. Getting Eve to imagine she was being deprived set the stage for satan's success. *"And the woman said unto the serpent, We may eat of the fruit of the trees of the garden: but of the fruit of the tree which is in the midst of the garden, God hath said, Ye shall not eat of it, neither shall ye touch it, lest ye die."*[6]

Adam failed to convey God's commandment accurately so Eve did not know exactly what God had said. Taking away the word *freely*, she added the phrase *"neither shall ye touch it."* Realizing the woman did not fully know God's ordinance, the serpent set up a full-scale attack on her selfish nature, seeking to make her succumb. *"And the serpent said unto the woman, Ye shall not surely die: for God doth know that in the day ye eat thereof, then your eyes shall be opened, and ye shall be as gods, knowing good and evil."*[7]

Zing! his missile penetrated her mind and

pierced her soul. Contemplating the benefits **she** would acquire from partaking of the forbidden fruit, Eve made the fatal decision of disobedience. *"And when the woman saw that the tree was good for food, and that it was pleasant to the eyes, and a tree to be desired to make one wise, she took of the fruit thereof, and did eat, and gave also unto her husband with her; and he did eat."*[8]

Contained within the original enticement of mankind are the three areas of temptation each person will face. *"For all that is in the world, the lust of the flesh, and the lust of the eyes, and the pride of life, is not of the Father, but is of the world."*[9] Every transgression falls into one of these categories and is a result of our lusts. Lust simply means **I want!**

Herein lies the root cause for sin—WE SIN BECAUSE WE ARE SELFISH!! *"But every man is tempted, when he is drawn away of his own lust, and enticed. Then when lust hath conceived, it bringeth forth sin: and sin, when it is finished, bringeth forth death. Do not err, my beloved brethren."*[10]

Lucifer's rebellion against God was rooted in pride resulting in his self-seeking passion for preeminence in the heavenly domain. Isaiah recorded the five "I will's" of his lustful heart. *"How art thou fallen*

117

*from heaven, O Lucifer, son of the morning! how art thou cut down to the ground, which didst weaken the nations! For thou hast said in thine heart, <u>I will</u> ascend into heaven, <u>I will</u> exalt my throne above the stars of God: <u>I will</u> sit also upon the mount of the congregation, in the sides of the north: <u>I will</u> ascend above the heights of the clouds; <u>I will</u> be like the most High.*"[11]

Satan's egotistical craving for supremacy continues to control his every move. Utilizing the same selfish appetites within the soulish nature of man, he manipulates and destroys humanity. After succumbing to self-seeking desires, another resident emerges in the kingdom of self–self-preservation. Return with me if you will to the scenario in the garden.

*"And they heard the voice of the LORD God walking in the garden in the cool of the day: <u>and Adam and his wife hid themselves</u> from the presence of the LORD God amongst the trees of the garden. And the LORD God called unto Adam, and said unto him, Where art thou?*"[12] Prior to their transgression, communion with their Creator was the most glorious privilege. Now the knowledge of good and evil filled Adam and Eve with fear. *"And he said, I heard thy voice in the garden, and <u>I was afraid</u>, because I was*

*naked; and I hid myself.*"[13]

"*And he said, Who told thee that thou wast na- ked? Hast thou eaten of the tree, whereof I com- manded thee that thou shouldest not eat?*"[14] At this point in the dialogue, self-preservation makes its grand entrance into the kingdom of self. *"And the man said, The woman whom thou gavest to be with me, she gave me of the tree, and I did eat. And the LORD God said unto the woman, What is this that thou hast done? And the woman said, The serpent beguiled me, and I did eat.*"[15] In an attempt to preserve them- selves, Adam blamed Eve and God while Eve blamed the serpent. As the old saying goes, "The devil made me do it."

To this day, self-preservation is the strongest force in the world. Humanity will engage in the most barbarous deeds in an effort to survive, even to the point of cannibalizing their own babies or family mem- bers. History is replete with horrific examples.

No one has to be taught how to function in this realm. It is inbred in each of us. From the cradle to the grave we become adept at blaming others for our misdeeds. In this modern day of justification, every- one is a victim of somebody else's mistakes. Even ne- farious criminals can plead insanity or blame their upbringing.

The soul is the seat of selfishness. That is why Jesus, the living Word, came to save our souls. *"Wherefore lay apart all filthiness and superfluity of naughtiness, and receive with meekness the engrafted word, which is able to <u>save your souls</u>."*[16]

In the Garden of Eden, the curse came. Nevertheless, in the Garden of Gethsemane, the curse was reversed. *"Then cometh Jesus with them unto a place called Gethsemane, and saith unto the disciples, Sit ye here, while I go and pray yonder. And he took with him Peter and the two sons of Zebedee, and began to be sorrowful and very heavy. Then saith he unto them, <u>My soul is exceeding sorrowful, even unto death</u>: tarry ye here, and watch with me. And he went a little further, and fell on his face, and prayed, saying, O my Father, if it be possible, let this cup pass from me: nevertheless not as I will, but as thou wilt. And he cometh unto the disciples, and findeth them asleep, and saith unto Peter, What, could ye not watch with me one hour? Watch and pray, that ye enter not into temptation: the spirit indeed is willing, but the flesh is weak. He went away again the second time, and prayed, saying, O my Father, if this cup may not pass away from me, except I drink it, thy will* *be done.* "[17]

Gethsemane's struggle took place in the realm of the soul. It was the human soul of the Messiah that wrestled with the submission to the cross. Self-preservation screamed for supremacy. *"Thinkest thou that I cannot now pray to my Father, and he shall presently give me more than twelve legions of angels? But how then shall the scriptures be fulfilled, that thus it must be?"*[18] Gethsemane, meaning *winepress*, extracted every ounce of self-preservation from the soul of the Master. This is where the battle was won. From that point, He was led as a lamb to the slaughter.

Calvary's sacrifice was much more than the crucifixion of a human body. It was the offering of His soul. *"Yet it pleased the LORD to bruise him; he hath put him to grief: when thou shalt <u>make his soul an offering for sin</u>, he shall see his seed, he shall prolong his days, and the pleasure of the LORD shall prosper in his hand. He shall see of <u>the travail of his soul</u>, and shall be satisfied: by his knowledge shall my righteous servant justify many; for he shall bear their iniquities. Therefore will I divide him a portion with the great, and he shall divide the spoil with the strong; because <u>he hath poured out his soul unto death</u>: and he was numbered with the transgressors;*

and he bare the sin of many, and made intercession
for the transgressors. "[19]

"Then said Jesus unto his disciples, If any man
will come after me, let him deny himself, and take up
his cross, and follow me."[20] His disciples must be
willing to deny themselves, take their crosses, and
walk the same pathway to the hill of crucifixion. Our
bodies will not be crucified but rather our self-seeking
natures that reign supreme in the kingdom of self.

Seven times the Word of God bids us to lose our
life so that we will find it:

➤ *"He that findeth his life shall lose it: and he
that loseth his life for my sake shall find it"*
(Matthew 10:39).

➤ *"For whosoever will save his life shall lose it:
and whosoever will lose his life for my sake
shall find it"* (Matthew 16:25).

➤ *"For whosoever will save his life shall lose it;
but whosoever shall lose his life for my sake
and the gospel's, the same shall save it"* (Mark
8:35).

➢ *"For whosoever will save his life shall lose it: but whosoever will lose his life for my sake, the same shall save it"* (Luke 9:24).

➢ *"If any man come to me, and hate not his father, and mother, and wife, and children, and brethren, and sisters, yea, and his own life also, he cannot be my disciple"* (Luke 14:26).

➢ *"Whosoever shall seek to save his life shall lose it; and whosoever shall lose his life shall preserve it"* (Luke 17:33).

➢ *"He that loveth his life shall lose it; and he that hateth his life in this world shall keep it unto life eternal"* (John 12:25).

The word *life* in all but one place in these Scriptures is the Greek word "pschue" *(psoo-khay)*. It is the exact same Greek word for *soul*, and these two words are used interchangeably. The life we must be willing to lose is our self-centered soul life. Then we will keep it unto *life eternal*. In this phrase, John referred to a different kind of life and used the Greek word "zoe" *(dzo-ay)* meaning spirit life. Sacrificing our soul life will produce eternal spirit life.

Daily the war rages within our inner man. *"This I say then, Walk in the Spirit, and ye shall not fulfil the lust of the flesh. For the flesh lusteth against the Spirit, and the Spirit against the flesh: and these are contrary the one to the other: so that ye cannot do the things that ye would."*[21] This is where the battle is either won or lost. The key to victory over the flesh lies in which nature you feed the most, the spiritual man or the carnal man.

Many years ago my father told me an old Indian parable that illustrates this principle. The spirit man resembles a white dog, the carnal man a black dog, which are in a constant battle in your inner man. Continually engaging in combat, the dog you feed the most will win the war. Which dog are you feeding the most? What kind of music, books, and entertainment do you feast on? Do you engage in the discipline of daily devotions and prayer? Remember the nature you nurture will control your appetites, bringing victory or defeat in the kingdom of self.

Ultimate surrender of self is found in being *"crucified with Christ."*[22] Paul said, *"I die daily."*[23] *"Verily, verily, I say unto you, Except a corn of wheat fall into the ground and die, it abideth alone: but if it die, it bringeth forth much fruit.*"[24] If Jesus had not gone to Calvary, the Spirit of God would have remained encapsulated within Him. Because he was willing to suffer and die, the Spirit was released on the Day of Pentecost, bringing forth much fruit. Putting to death our soul life and releasing the Holy Spirit will bear fruit unto life eternal not only in us but also in the world around us.

Will you answer the clarion call to crucify the carnal man? Are you ready to sacrifice the greatest idol in your life? "I see the face of a god and I raise this god over the earth, who will grant them joy and peace and pride. This god, this one word: **I**." This is the last god to go and it will only meet its demise on Moriah's lonely summit of sacrifice. When self has been dethroned from the kingdom of your soul the scepter of sovereignty will be truly transferred to the King of kings.

In my heart are kingdoms of a world that's all
my own
Kingdoms that are only seen by myself and God
alone
In the past when I tried to rule my world,

it just seemed to fall apart
So please Jesus be the Lord
of all the kingdoms of my heart

I guess I only fooled myself for I said I had
yielded all
But in a secret corner of my heart was a
kingdom that did not fall
I surrender now, make my heart Your throne
rule its kingdoms great and small
FOR IF YOU'RE NOT LORD OF
EVERYTHING
THEN YOU'RE NOT LORD AT ALL![25]

## Chapter Eleven Footnotes:

1. I Peter 2:9

2. II Peter 3:18

3. Genesis 2:7

4. Genesis 2:16-17

5. Genesis 3:1

6. Genesis 3:2-3

7. Genesis 3:4-5

8. Genesis 3:6

9. I John 2:16

10. James 1:14-16

11. Isaiah 14:12-14

12. Genesis 3:8-9

13. Genesis 3:10

14. Genesis 3:11

15. Genesis 3:12-13

16. James 1:21

17. Matthew 26:36-42

18. Matthew 26:53-54

19. Isaiah 53:10-12

20. Matthew 16:24

21. Galatians 5:16-17

22. Galatians 2:20

23. I Corinthians 15:31

24. John 12:24

25. "Jesus Be the Lord of All," Lanny and Marietta Wolfe  (copyright 1975 by Lanny Wolfe Music Co.)

# "Gather My Saints"

*By faith Abraham, when he was called to go out into a place which he should after receive for an inheritance, obeyed; and he went out, not knowing whither he went. By faith he sojourned in the land of promise, as in a strange country, dwelling in tabernacles with Isaac and Jacob, the heirs with him of the same promise: <u>for he looked for a city which hath foundations, whose builder and maker is God.</u>*"[1]

Abraham was the first man to break out of the age-old rhythm of cyclical thinking. Believing eternal life was available only to the gods, the ancients thought mankind could only look forward to the finality of death. For them, happiness was found in the daily pursuit of pleasure. They lived to eat, dance, play, and have material blessings. Nevertheless, in the midst of such mindless beliefs, Abraham destroyed the paradigm by setting his sights on a city whose builder and maker is God. Traveling the road of relationship with the Almighty infused him with a new way of thinking and experiencing life. With each sacrifice the shackles of his former life fell away and he discovered hope beyond this vale of tears.

Much like the archaic mind-set of Mesopotamia, modern peoples have reverted to the same mode of thinking. Like a certain rich man in Luke 12, they espouse the age-old philosophy of eating, drinking, and making merry. Caught up in materialistic goals and the quest for riches, many focus on the vapor of a lifetime. Never investing in eternal treasures leaves them with no hope beyond this mortal life. *"So is he that layeth up treasure for himself, and is not rich toward God."²*

Apostle Paul reminds us, *"If in this life only we have hope in Christ, we are of all men most miserable."³* Breaking out of the futile pattern of selfish pursuits and embarking on the road of relationship with God enable us to experience life at its best. Mortifying the flesh transforms our thinking, empowering us to set our affection on things above and not on the earth. We have the best of both worlds–a blessed earthly existence and assurance of eternal life. *"And every one that hath forsaken houses, or brethren, or sisters, or father, or mother, or wife, or children, or lands, for my name's sake, shall receive an hundredfold, and shall inherit everlasting life."*[4]

*"These all died in faith, not having received the promises, but having seen them afar off, and were persuaded of them, and embraced them, and confessed that they were strangers and pilgrims on the earth. For they that say such things declare plainly that they seek a country. And truly, if they had been mindful of that country from whence they came out, they might have had opportunity to have returned."*[5]  Looking back at the world causes some sojourners to scoff at the necessity of walking a road paved with sacrifice.  Gradually descending into the old life of sin, many seem oblivious to the destruction of their relationship with God.

Without exception the message of liberty is loudly proclaimed.  Nonetheless, it is not the freedom of a liberated life in Jesus but the liberty of release from the pressure of standing strong in the warfare against sin.  Since they have succumbed to the temptation of worldliness offered by satan, he no longer battles against them.  Believing their lack of consecration is pleasing to God, they avidly promote a "liberated" lifestyle.

Peter declared, *"While they promise them liberty, they themselves are the servants of corruption: for of whom a man is overcome, of the same is he brought in bondage. For if after they have escaped the pollutions of the world through the knowledge of the Lord and Saviour Jesus Christ, they are again entangled therein, and overcome, the latter end is worse with them than the beginning. For it had been better for them not to have known the way of righteousness, than, after they have known it, to turn from the holy commandment delivered unto them. But it is happened unto them according to the true proverb, The dog is turned to his own vomit again; and the sow that was washed to her wallowing in the mire.*[6]

When the sacrifice of sanctification is removed, one's salvation message becomes polluted. Invariably this happens because these two issues are inseparably linked. *"Who is he that overcometh the world, but he that believeth that Jesus is the Son of God?"*[7] Ceasing to overcome the world obfuscates one's comprehension of the mighty God in Christ. Next, the fundamental plan of salvation set forth in Acts 2:38 is no longer deemed necessary. Sadly, some preachers have publicly apologized for espousing these doctrines in the past.

Paul warned Timothy, *"If any man teach otherwise, and consent not to wholesome words, even the words of our Lord Jesus Christ, and to the doctrine which is according to godliness; he is proud, knowing nothing, but doting about questions and strifes of words, whereof cometh envy, strife, railings, evil surmisings, perverse disputings of men of corrupt minds, and destitute of the truth, supposing that gain is godliness: from such withdraw thyself.*"[8]

Forsaking a separated lifestyle and equating gain with godliness, many deceive themselves into thinking obedience to God's precepts is no longer necessary. We must never forget, even in this "enlightened" age, obeying the doctrine of the apostles, *"which is according to godliness,"* is heaven's admission ticket. *"Dearly beloved, I beseech you as strangers and pilgrims, abstain from fleshly lusts, which war against the soul."*[9]

Hebrews 12:14 states, *"Follow peace with all men, and holiness, without which no man shall see the Lord."* Let us consider the three "sees" contained in this Scripture. Mirroring His holy image will allow people to "see" the Lord, for we are epistles known and read of all men. Holiness also enables us to "see" or perceive God correctly. Lastly, following holiness makes it possible to "see" the Lord in peace on that great day.

*"But now they desire a better country, that is, an heavenly: wherefore God is not ashamed to be called their God: for he hath prepared for them a city."*[10]

133

Departing from Haran, Abraham never looked back. To the end of his life, he continued to desire a better country. Pulling back the curtain of time and peering into the future, the Word of God reveals the supreme fulfillment of Abraham's quest. *"And I say unto you, That many shall come from the east and west, and shall sit down with Abraham, and Isaac, and Jacob, in the kingdom of heaven."*[11]

Likewise, gaining eternal life is the ultimate conclusion of our covenant pilgrimage. *"Nevertheless we, according to his promise, look for new heavens and a new earth, wherein dwelleth righteousness."*[12]

The psalmist wrote about this glorious assurance, *"Our God shall come, and shall not keep silence: a fire shall devour before him, and it shall be very tempestuous round about him. He shall call to the heavens from above, and to the earth, that he may judge his people. Gather my saints together unto me; those that have made a covenant with me by sacrifice."*[13]

One day we will all stand before the judgment seat of Christ, and a personal covenant by sacrifice will be the essential element in gaining entrance into the everlasting kingdom. *"Wherefore the rather, brethren, give diligence to make your calling and election sure: for if ye do these things, ye shall never fall: for so an entrance shall be ministered unto you abundantly into the everlasting kingdom of our Lord and Saviour Jesus Christ."*[14] Is your greatest hope to have an abundant entrance and sit down with Abraham in the kingdom of heaven? *"And every man that hath this hope in him purifieth himself, even as he is pure."*[15] Your sacrifices will determine your destiny!

*"Gather my saints together unto me; those that have made a covenant with me by sacrifice. And the heavens shall declare his righteousness: <u>for God is judge himself.</u> Selah."*[16] Pause and think about it. . . .

It will be worth it all, when we see Jesus
Life's trials will seem so small,
when we see Christ
One glimpse of His dear face,
All sorrow will erase,
So bravely run the race
TILL WE SEE CHRIST![17]

## <u>Epilogue Footnotes:</u>

1. Hebrews 11:8-10

2. Luke 12:21

3. I Corinthians 15:19

4. Matthew 19:29

5. Hebrews 11:13-15

6. II Peter 2:19-22

7. I John 5:5

8. I Timothy 6:3-5

9. I Peter 2:11

10. Hebrews 11:16

11. Matthew 8:11

12. II Peter 3:13

13. Psalm 50:3-5

14. II Peter 1:10-11

15. I John 3:3

16. Psalm 50:5-6

17. "When We See Christ," Esther Kerr Rusthoi, copyright 1941

# Reference Bibliography

Almighty God. *The Holy Bible.*

*The Amplified Bible, Expanded Edition.* Zondervan.

Cahill, Thomas. *The Gifts of the Jews.* Nan A. Talese / Anchor Books, Doubleday.

Henry, Matthew, Thomas Scott. *Matthew Henry Commentary.* Thomas Nelson Publishers, Nashville–Camden–New York.

Hoerth, Alfred J. *Archaeology and the Old Testament.* Baker Books, A division of Baker Book House Co., Grand Rapids, MI.

Kaiser, Walter C., Jr. *A History of Israel, From the Bronze Age through the Jewish Wars.* Broadman and Holman Publishers, Nashville, TN.

Knight, Walter B. *Knight's Master Book of New Illustrations.* Wm. B. Eerdmans Publishing Company, Grand Rapids, MI.

Meyer, F. B. *The Life of Abraham.* Emerald Books, Lynwood, WA.

Packer, J. I., M. C. Tenney. *Illustrated Manners and Customs of the Bible.* Thomas Nelson Publishers, Nashville, TN.

Strong, James, S.T.D., LL.D. *Abingdon's Strong's Exhaustive Concordance of the Bible.* Abingdon, Nashville.

Traylor, Ellen Gunderson. *The Song of Abraham.* Tyndale House Publishers, Inc., Wheaton, IL.

Unger, Merrill F., Th.D., Ph.D. *Unger's Bible Dictionary.* Moody Press, Chicago.

*Webster's New Reference Library.* A Nelson/Regency Publication, Thomas Nelson Publishers, Nashville –Camden–New York.